U0042676

諸君所見，非名勝古蹟。

WHAT YOU SEE ARE NOT
HISTORIC MONUMENTS.

無所不在
無神不拜
無孔不入
無奇不有

UBIQUITOUS
POLYTHEISTIC
PERVASIVE
WONDROUS

PARASITIC
TEMPLES

台灣都市夾縫中的街廟觀察
適應社會變遷的常民空間圖鑑

賴伯威◎著
WillipodiA都市研究團隊

野人

目錄
Contents

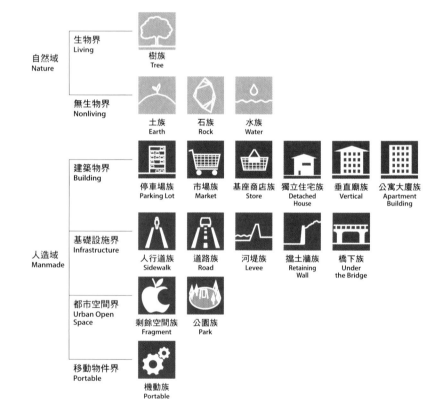

自然域 Nature	生物界 Living	樹族 Tree			
	無生物界 Nonliving	土族 Earth	石族 Rock	水族 Water	
人造域 Manmade	建築物界 Building	停車場族 Parking Lot	市場族 Market	基座商店族 Store	獨立住宅族 Detached House	垂直廟族 Vertical	公寓大廈族 Apartment Building
	基礎設施界 Infrastructure	人行道族 Sidewalk	道路族 Road	河堤族 Levee	擋土牆族 Retaining Wall	橋下族 Under the Bridge
	都市空間界 Urban Open Space	剩餘空間族 Fragment	公園族 Park			
	移動物件界 Portable	機動族 Portable				

6 | 廟等角透視圖：36+1案例
Isometric Diagrams

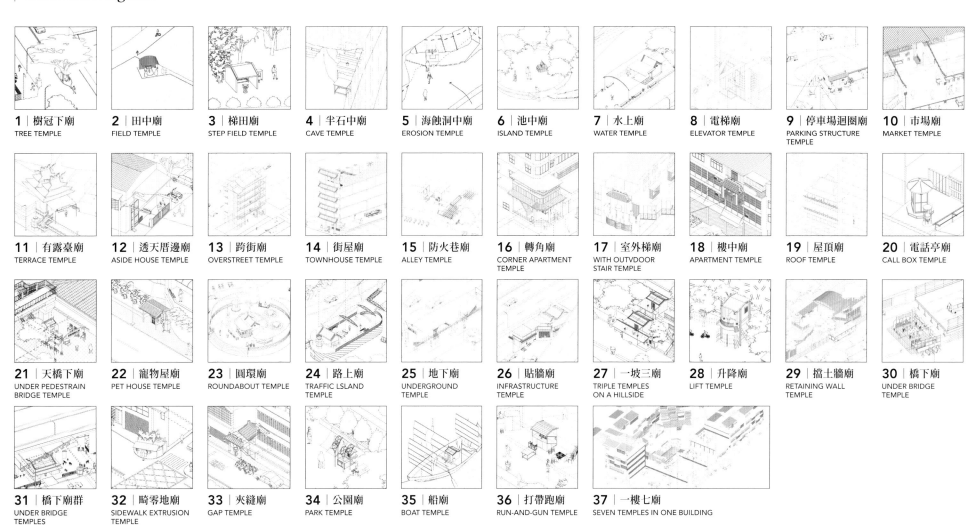

1 | 樹冠下廟
TREE TEMPLE

2 | 田中廟
FIELD TEMPLE

3 | 梯田廟
STEP FIELD TEMPLE

4 | 半石中廟
CAVE TEMPLE

5 | 海蝕洞中廟
EROSION TEMPLE

6 | 池中廟
ISLAND TEMPLE

7 | 水上廟
WATER TEMPLE

8 | 電梯廟
ELEVATOR TEMPLE

9 | 停車場迴圈廟
PARKING STRUCTURE TEMPLE

10 | 市場廟
MARKET TEMPLE

11 | 有露臺廟
TERRACE TEMPLE

12 | 透天厝邊廟
ASIDE HOUSE TEMPLE

13 | 跨街廟
OVERSTREET TEMPLE

14 | 街屋廟
TOWNHOUSE TEMPLE

15 | 防火巷廟
ALLEY TEMPLE

16 | 轉角廟
CORNER APARTMENT TEMPLE

17 | 室外梯廟
WITH OUTVDOOR STAIR TEMPLE

18 | 樓中廟
APARTMENT TEMPLE

19 | 屋頂廟
ROOF TEMPLE

20 | 電話亭廟
CALL BOX TEMPLE

21 | 天橋下廟
UNDER PEDESTRAIN BRIDGE TEMPLE

22 | 寵物屋廟
PET HOUSE TEMPLE

23 | 圓環廟
ROUNDABOUT TEMPLE

24 | 路上廟
TRAFFIC LSLAND TEMPLE

25 | 地下廟
UNDERGROUND TEMPLE

26 | 貼牆廟
INFRASTRUCTURE TEMPLE

27 | 一坡三廟
TRIPLE TEMPLES ON A HILLSIDE

28 | 升降廟
LIFT TEMPLE

29 | 擋土牆廟
RETAINING WALL TEMPLE

30 | 橋下廟
UNDER BRIDGE TEMPLE

31 | 橋下廟群
UNDER BRIDGE TEMPLES

32 | 畸零地廟
SIDEWALK EXTRUSION TEMPLE

33 | 夾縫廟
GAP TEMPLE

34 | 公園廟
PARK TEMPLE

35 | 船廟
BOAT TEMPLE

36 | 打帶跑廟
RUN-AND-GUN TEMPLE

37 | 一樓七廟
SEVEN TEMPLES IN ONE BUILDING

起點：回到故鄉才能開始的事

The origin: A project can only be started in my hometown

在多年的四處漂泊中，不斷有這樣的錯覺：「故鄉」與「他鄉」的界線模糊到幾乎不存在。哪裡是歸處？哪裡算是歸處？回家，感覺只是另一場旅行，沒有「故鄉」與「他鄉」的分別，與其說是台灣人，不如說更像地球人。

多年來，走過、工作過、生活過台灣以外的許多城市，回到故鄉時，才能換一種類外來者的視角再一次認識自己熟悉的城市。有感於台灣文化資源依然尚待挖掘、與同時認清我們唯一所擁有的，便是家中的敝帚，然而自珍的態度，是可以選擇的。

因這樣的文化自覺，嘗試用建築人的專業，去重新解讀、記錄，透過這108種不同的台灣都市環境與廟的結合關係呈現台灣都市最具特色的那一部分給世界。

這是回到故鄉才能開始的事！

違建意外成為都市奇觀與基因

回溯這個念頭的觸發點，那是2010年，我參加當時任職的上海AECOM環境規劃公司主辦的台北萬華工作營中，偶然地發現了萬華水濂宮，此廟與其說是「夾」在環河南路橋下與環河快速道路下的河堤牆之間，倒不如說「寄生」在橋下與河堤牆間。面對這樣的現象，我心想：若說這不是違建，那什麼算違建？但它卻如此堂而皇之地「不合理」地存在著。再細細探究，像水濂宮

這樣的違建廟比比皆是，它們因應社會變遷而瘦身變形、因神明「指示」而改變路況地貌、因居民「想要」而有保留的理由……違建的形式多元而有創意，似乎成了台灣都市識別度最高的「都市性狀」——台灣都市地景的基因。

不是尋找「為什麼」
只在記錄「是什麼」

2013年回台後，我成立了WillipodiA都市研究團隊，和一群同好、學生、台灣人、外國人、朋友的朋友、九典事務所的同事……開始漫長的「寄生之廟」都市觀察記錄。這本書記錄的核心是以廟為載體，然而廟的故事與歷史並不是最重要的，重要的是它們依然存在的當下，記錄著這時代的需求與都市周邊紋理。

此研究紀錄的起點，我或多或少受到兩位前輩的影響，一是在波士頓留學時的老師，塚本由晴的著作《東京製造》；二是在上海工作時，亦師亦友的同事，筱原寬之的研究《城市自訂車》。在台灣WillipodiA團隊主要的工作內容是收集「寄生之廟」案例、描述寄生狀況、命名、分類、編目與繪圖。我們不著重找出這些廟存在的普遍性宗教解釋，而是關注於廟體存在現象與事實的個別性與獨特性。我們嘗試將在台灣四處蒐集來的廟——如寄生生物一般的

寄生之廟，建立如生物分類般的分類總表與其在水泥叢林中廟的演化。過程中也發現，許多新一代在都市中的廟已逐漸往「只具有廟的功能，而不具備廟的外形」演化，至少不再是我們傳統上所認知廟的外形。但受限於有限的人力物力，在108種台灣寄生之廟的種類中我們只能挑選了36種外加一個特別的混合案例放進此書，很多精彩有趣的廟不免成為遺珠。

我們所做的一切，不是換一個視角或觀點看這些廟與這些城市切片，而是從先換一種表達方式切入，透過這樣的解讀與詮釋，去表達存在這塊土地上的事物與現象依然可以有其深度與代表台灣的獨特性，如《清明上河圖》曾經還原宋代都市般，這些紀錄圖紙是台灣當今都市型態與生活樣貌的浮世繪。

記錄本身即為價值。

回歸現象本身已存在的事實

無論寄生之廟算是城市之美還是城市之醜，我們都覺得應該跳脫表象的美醜，回歸到「現象就是現象」，因其無可否認「已存在」的事實，它呈現的是所有不合理的事件與不合理的因子加總後得到的最合理結果。

我們的關注的不是現象背後的本質，而是現象本身。

不追究其原因、原理、原則，只因記錄從而知道：
　　這樣的文化
　　這樣的經濟
　　這樣的社會
　　這樣的環境
　　這樣的政府
　　這樣的人民

林林總總加起來得到的就是：
　　這樣的城市
　　這樣的現象
　　這樣的結果

「寄生之廟」為「往生之間」、「重生之路」這三本書中的第一本。謹以此書，喚起我們自己對日常生活周遭環境的觀察與重視，特別是那些視而不見或習以為常的部分。就好比這些一直存在你我身邊的寄生之廟。

再一次重新地
認識台灣

感謝一路走來所有付出的人

Throughout the many years of wandering all over the world, I keep having the misconception that the boundaries between "hometown" and "foreign places" are so blurred that do not seem to exist. Where is the place to return? Where can be considered as a place to return? Coming home feels like just another journey. The demarcation between hometown and other places no longer exists. Instead of calling myself a Taiwanese, "Earthling" could be a more appropriate name.

Over the years, I have been to, work and live in many cities outside of Taiwan. When I come back, I am able to re-familiarize myself with the cities I already know from a foreign perspective. Feeling that the cultural resources of Taiwan is still to be discovered, and at the same time recognizing the only treasure we have is what we own, we, however, can acquire the attitude of appreciating them.

To this cultural self-awareness, I try to use the expertise of the architecture profession, through studying the 108 types of connecting relationships between Taiwanese urban environment and the temples, to reanalyze and record the 36 cases and 1 special case, and show the most characteristic part of Taiwan to the world.

This is a project can only be started in my hometown!

Illegal buildings accidentally become urban wonders and genes

When I worked at AECOM Shanghai office in 2010, I participated in a workshop held by the firm in Wanhua, Taipei, where I discovered Shuilian Temple by chance. Rather than describing it to be caught between the Huanhe South Road overpass and the levee under New Taipei Huanhe Expressway, it is even more accurate to say that it "parasitizes" between the overpass and the levee. Seeing this, I could not help thinking, "If this is not an illegal building, what is an illegal building?" It, however, unreasonably exists in broad daylight. With some research, it is not hard to find that illegally built temples like Shuilian Temple are everywhere. They transform in response to social changes, alter the streetscape under the deities' directions, or have been preserved due to the community's needs. The forms of illegally built temples are varied and creative, which seem to become the most identifiable feature of Taiwanese cities, the gene of Taiwanese urban landscapes.

Not researching "why" but documenting "what"

After returning to Taiwan in 2013, I founded Willipodia, an urban research team, collaborating with my fellow aficionados, students, Taiwanese and foreigners, and friends of friends, to start a long journey of documenting unban parasite temples. While focusing on the temples, this book also covers their local urban folk cultures. In fact, our team found that the meaning of these temples, in terms of urban taxonomy, is endowed by their surrounding environment. Each temple is a puzzle piece of a city, recording what happened in the city corners and exemplifying the characters of Taiwanese cities' genes.

To some extent, this research was inspired by two of my mentors. One is the coauthor of *Made in Tokyo*, Tsukamoto Yoshiharu, my teacher in Harvard. The other is the author of *Custom Bike Urbanism*, Shinohara Hiroyuki, my colleague when I worked in Shanghai, who was both a teacher and a friend to me. The main mission of WillipodiA is to collect cases of parasite temples, describe their parasitic conditions, name, classify, catalogue and map them. We do not aim to find their common religious explanations, but to emphasize the individuality and uniqueness of their physical existence. We try to treat these temples, collected from all over Taiwan, as living creatures, and design a taxonomy like its biological counterpart to trace their evolution within the concrete jungle. During the process, we found many new urban temples have gradually evolved into those which only carry the function but not the forms of temples. Due to manpower and resource limitations, we had to select 36+1 special out of the 108 kinds of parasite temples in Taiwan to be visualized in this book.

What we have done is not simply looking at these temples and urban biopsy from a different perspective, but utilizing a different method to probe and, with this new interpretation, to demonstrate that the things and phenomena on this island do have their depth and the uniqueness to represent Taiwan. Just like the famous painting *Along the River During the Qingming Festival*, which reveals urban lives in the Song dynasty, our documentary is an ukiyo-e of urban lifestyles in modern Taiwan. How invaluable it is!

Return to the fact of their existence

While parasite temples may be regarded as a city's beauty or otherwise, we should look beyond their appearance and focus on the undeniable truth of their existence, which is the most reasonable outcome of all unreasonable events and factors.

What we are concerned about is not the nature of the phenomenon but the phenomenon itself. We do not have to dig into it, because the final outcome, the phenomenon and the cities are contingent on the culture, the economy, the society, the environment, the people and the government.

Parasite Temples is the first volume of a trilogy. I hope this book can urge us to observe and value our everyday surroundings, especially those are taken for granted or deliberately ignored, like these ever-existing parasite temples around us.

Let's get to know Taiwan all over again.

Special thanks to all those who have contributed their efforts along the way

1

緣起
The Origin

台灣都市夾縫中的廟，
是台灣城市
有別於世界其他地方
最顯而易見的與眾不同，
這些宛如寄生在都市的廟：

這些廟，是真實的台灣印象
這些廟，是沒有建築師的建築
這些廟，沒沒無聞，名不見經傳
這些廟，是顯而易見的都市基因
這些廟，本身存在的事實即為現象
這些廟，是常民對現實生活的避風港
這些廟，隱身街頭巷尾，你家我家之間
這些廟，曾見證老百姓資本的高度集中
這些廟，都市的縮影，社會變遷的活化石
這些廟，是最能赤裸反映台灣都市的獨特性
這些廟，是常民建築，直接效率經濟才是解答
這些廟，未來都市的發展將不再有它們的存在
這些廟，普遍出現在台灣都市的各個夾縫與角落
這些廟，絕大多數不是如建築模範生般的文化大廟
這些廟，展現了台灣人合法或不合法適應環境的韌性
這些廟，是沒有設計教育汙染而不刻意設計出來的設計
這些廟，多處在荒謬離譜的基地，出沒於都市的各個角落
這些廟，有強烈信仰寄託與情感需求的那一代已隨時間凋零
這些廟，是成長環境中我們習以為常，或者有人選擇視而不見
這些廟，整個都市都是它們的宿主，寄生於台灣的都市環境中
這些廟，因宗教信仰的不可侵犯而能遊走法律邊緣與情感的鄉愿
這些廟，嵌入都市建築中的常民智慧而激發出神奇的空間組合關係
這些廟，除了宗教上意義，也扮演著社區裡老人生活聚會的集會場所
這些廟，曾與某年代的台灣人日常生活密不可分，是社區與鄰里的核心
這些廟，大多不符合現代建築美學標準，卻絕對符合神人供需關係的必然
這些廟，不是想像，而是在台灣都市的水泥叢林中自然生長演化出來的生物
這些廟，生活在都市的年輕世代，對於美好城市的想像，不再有它們的存在
這些廟，曾是台灣人民真正想要的有形欲望，是欲望以空間與建築呈現的面貌

The temples in the urban gaps are
what make Taiwan cities significantly different
from their counterparts around the world.
These temples are like urban parasites.

They are true impressions of Taiwan.
They are buildings with no architects.
They are not prominent or famous.
They are obvious genes of a city.
Their very existence is a phenomenon.
They are common people's shelter from real life.
They hide in the streets and alleys among our houses.
They witnessed a high concentration of people's capital.
They are the epitome of a city, living fossils of social change.
They best reflect the uniqueness of Taiwan cities.
They are common people's buildings, representing direct and efficient economy.
They will no longer exist in a city's future development.
They are common in gaps and corners among Taiwan cities.
They are usually small, not model buildings to demonstrate cultures.
They show the Taiwanese's toughness, legal or not, to adapt to the environment.
They are designed unintentionally, not contaminated by design education.
They are usually located in absurd sites, appearing in every possible corner of a city.
They are the faith center and emotional need of a generation fading away with time.
They are taken for granted or deliberately ignored.
They, taking the whole city as their host, are parasitic in Taiwan cities.
They are in a gray area of justice and morality because of the inviolability of religious beliefs.
They, embedded with common people's wisdom, spark off a marvelous space combination.
They, aside from their religious meaning, are rendezvous of community seniors.
They, as the core of a community or neighborhood, were once closely tied to the Taiwanese of a certain era.
They are usually not in accordance with modern architectural aesthetics, but comply with the necessity of urban supply and demand.
They are not imagination but creatures evolving from the concrete jungle of Taiwan cities.
They no longer exist in the urban younger generation's imagination of a perfect city.
They were once tangible desires of the Taiwanese when desires could be represented in space through architecture.

它們為數眾多，大隱於市。
一些廟在其周邊日漸變化的
都市環境下越顯越小，
收縮到只占據最極限的
都市空間；一些廟則在
都市化過程中留下的
剩餘空間尋找夾縫求生，
融合並嵌入都市與
常民建築的某個角落：

在橋下、
在圓環中、
在屋頂上、
跨越街道、
長出輪子、
小到一個箱子、
大至一棟高樓。

They are numerous, hidden
in the cities. As the urban
environment develops,
some temples become
smaller and smaller, shrinking
to only occupy minimal urban
space. Others struggle in the
gaps left during urbanization,
embedded in some corners
between old and new
buildings:

Under bridges,
Within roundabouts,
Across streets,
With wheels,
As small as a box,
As tall as a high-rise.

人的生活場域本因著需求而產生構築行為，這些因應需求的構築行為的集合體則形成了城市。一間一間廟的存在，便反映了一次一次人類因應精神需求而產生的構築行為，無形精神需求的有形實體化呈現即為廟之本體。

然而今日城市會因更多的現代化需求而變遷革新；於是城市中已形成的構築個體，都必須因應大環境的轉變與發展，隨之演化而消失、新生或重生。在這無形信仰的需求仍被需要，但都市土地卻無法負荷，尺寸之地作為信仰之用，儼然已成為奢侈的情況下，人民所構築之廟便會因應著外部都市環境而改變、而轉化、而寄生——看似寄生。

多年來走過、工作過、生活過台灣以外的許多城市，回來時才能換一種外來者的視角再一次認識自己熟悉的城市。WillipodiA寄生之廟的觀察與記錄團隊幾年來收集了上百案例和廟與都市的結合關係，同時如影隨形揮之不去的問題是：

寄生之廟所聚焦記錄的這些廟到底算是城市中的美學抑或是醜學？

不得不承認，在歐美等已開發國家城市為主流美學價值的薰陶下，目前確實很難宣告台灣這些不具成為文化與建築典範的無名之廟，其寄生城市空間的現象可以被稱為一種美學。對此我們只能回歸現象本身已存在的事實：

無論歸於是城市之美或城市之醜，現象就是現象，所有不合理的事件與不合理的因子加總後得到的最合理的結果。現象本身，是不論美醜的。

探討寄生廟存在背後的成因，雖然很難抽離宗教信仰因素，但WillipodiA只想聚焦在都市觀察，點到為止即可，畢竟關於宗教信仰的討論已是另一門專業。

Needs urge people to construct, and the consequent constructions congregate to form a city. The embodiment of people's spiritual needs is temples. Therefore, the existence of each temple reflects a construction urged by spiritual needs.

Today, cities continue to change due to expanding modern needs. The existing buildings in the cities then also have to change according to the growing environment they are in, to disappear, to be relocated, or to be transformed. While the need for spiritual faith is still indispensable, there is not enough room in the city to meet the requirement. Using valuable lands to satisfy spiritual needs becomes a luxury. To respond to the changing urban environment, temples have to develop, to transform, or to parasitize (seemingly).

Having been to, worked in or lived in many cities outside Taiwan for years, I get the opportunity able to know the once familiar cities again with a pair of a foreigner's eyes. The WillipodiA parasitic temple team have collected hundreds of cases showing the relationship between temples and cities. The shadowing questions are: whether WillipodiA's documenting these temples is discovering a city's beauty or otherwise.

I have to admit that according to the western mainstream aesthetic values of developed country cities, it is difficult to claim that the phenomenon of these unknown temples' parasitizing in the urban space of Taiwan can be called a kind of aesthetics. So far, we can only look at its very own existence. Whether it is seen as a city's beauty or not, it is what it is, the most reasonable outcome of all unreasonable events and factors. The phenomenon itself is not about good- or bad-looking.

When it comes to the causes of a parasitic temple, religious factors are hard to ignore. This area will briefly be touched because WillipodiA just aim to focus on the observation of a city. After all, the discussion of religion is another field of knowledge.

What makes them survive in every city corner in their marvelous ways is their uniqueness and sanctity, the religious signatures these temples possess.

寄生之廟所處環境荒謬離譜的有趣，當然並不足以讓它們被保存於推土機外，而是廟具備宗教信仰的獨特性與神聖不可侵犯的特徵，讓它們以無奇不有的方式存在於都市的各個角落。若換作是其他用途的違建早就不復存在。它們遊走法律邊緣與情感上的鄉愿，它們不具備今日建築管理上的正當性，也不具備空間使用的正義，就法律而言更是侵占了公共利益與空間。

但法律之外，它們的存在保障了需要它們的族群的利益與空間，情感上的鄉愿讓建管單位不得不默許它們的存在。然而當傳統民間信仰已非生活必需的一部分、當老一輩凋零後，這種存在於都市角落的宗教空間是否還會存在？過去它們肩負著非宗教的其他功能早被今日的里民活動中心、里長辦公室、社區公園等其他形式的空間所取代。

這些廟日後會消失抑或繼續以這種怪誕的姿態存活下去？對此我不樂觀，因為自我以後的世代，對美好生活的需要與對美好都市的想像，並無這些廟的存在。需要它們的世代逐漸凋零，會是它們難以永遠在台灣都市立足的主因。但當它們逐漸消失，我們需要呼籲文資保存單位急救維護？還是聽任其符合演化定律自然淘汰、自然滅絕？我們無法回答，所以我們先作紀錄，用一個客觀的角度切入，採用中性的敘述，不帶批判的同思來看待台灣的都市，並用自己的角度、用有別於西方都市規劃的觀點來閱讀城市。

多年來旅外的生活經驗與工作閱歷，促使我不斷思考：台灣是否正處於劣質的都市與建築文化中？我想遺憾的是，答案很是肯定的。但這個觀察記錄的另一層意義是我選擇的，也只能擁抱它，擁抱你我觸目所及的，你我所共有的。

If they do not serve religious purpose, these "unapproved constructions" would have been removed. These temples wonder on the brinks of law and sentiment. Do they comply with construction management? No. Do they justify their use of space? No. Legally speaking, they bluntly infringe upon the public interests and invade public space.

Regardless of the law, the existence of these temples guarantees the interests and space of people in need, and the administration cannot help but acquiesce to the status quo. However, as the old generation perishes and the traditional folk religion is no longer a bare necessity of life, will this kind of religious space that scatters around the city continue to exist? The non-religious parts they used to play have been replaced by many other kinds of space, like community centers, village offices, or neighborhood parks. Will these temples fade away or survive in their bizarre ways? Personally, I am not optimistic about their future, because these temples are not part of necessities of comfortable lives nor imagination of a beautiful city for generations from mine on. It is difficult for these temples to have a place in the cities in Taiwan because the generations which need them are dying. Do we need to appeal for the preservation of cultural heritage, or allow them to be eliminated through natural selection? This is a question we are not able to answer. We choose to document it, seeing it with objectivity, describing it with neutrality, thinking without criticism about how to view cities in Taiwan and read them in one's own angle, which is different from the viewpoint of western urban planners.

Do years of living and working abroad tell me that Taiwan is really in the midst of poor urban and architectural culture? I think the answer is, sadly, positive. The other meaning of this observation report is that it is my own choice, and I feel obligated to embrace what we see and what we share.

陳植棋（1906－1931）〈街頭廟口〉
「人生是短促的，藝術才是永遠。」

Temple Front on the Street, Chen Zhiqi (1906 – 1931).
"Life is short. Art is forever."
感謝東之畫廊提供 Courtesy of East Gallery

台灣地景的基因

　　日本水彩家石川欽一郎首度將台灣本土的美表現出來後，開啟了台灣學子以自己的眼睛注視自己的鄉土，描繪鄉土的第一印象。他的學生們日後也成為台灣最重要的第一代西畫名家。他們開始自覺性的描繪台灣的地景，無論是使何種媒材，其畫的主題少不了廟，廟的建築顏色延伸到了描繪地景時的用色，廟的色彩即為台灣土地的色彩。

　　著名建築史學家梁思成對中國建築最大的貢獻，並非在於設計與建造任何建築，而是用西方建築圖學的方式與視角，來記錄中國自己的建築。他在美國求學時看到了《弗萊徹建築史》（*Sir Banister Fletcher's A History of Architecture*）後，與助手莫宗江測繪編寫《古建製圖》這部巨作。

　　本書受到兩位大師的啟發，採用現代建築學描述都市圖學的方式來記錄台灣自己的都市，以廟載體，延伸到其周邊。事實上我們研究團隊發現：這些廟在都市分類學的意義大多是其周邊環境賦予的，屬於台灣的都市基因。

Genes of Taiwan's Landscapes

After Kinichiro Ishikawa, a Japanese watercolor painter, first showed the local beauty of Taiwan, the Taiwanese were encouraged to watch their own land carefully and to draw their first impressions of it. Kinichiro's students later became some of the most prominent first-generation western painting masters in Taiwan. They started to depict Taiwan's landscapes, and no matter what material they used, temples were the major theme of their paintings. The colors of the temples expanded to the landscape; that is, the colors of the temples represented the colors of Taiwan's land.

Liang Sicheng's greatest contribution to Chinese architecture is not designing or building any construction, but documenting Chinese buildings with western architecture graphics. After reading *Sir Banister Fletcher' A History of Architecture*, Liang and his assistant, Mo Zongjiang, mapped and edited the masterpiece, *Gu Jian Zhi Tu*.

This book adopts modern architecture's way of mapping urban graphics to record Taiwan's cities, with temples in the center then everything around them. In fact, from our point of view, the meaning of these temples in urban taxonomy is fulfilled by their periphery, the genes of Taiwan's landscapes.

2

廟之所以為廟
The Definition
of Temple

物相化的宗教符號

　　宗教建築是宗教在俗世的物相化表現，一種絕對特化的建築類型，無論將其視為場所或物件，皆是被意識形態所特化的建築，很容易發展為「四處皆然」普世通用的形態，至少是能被信徒所廣泛接受與理解的形態，甚至為了強化其精神性而必須刻意弱化其生活性，或多或少創造出某種「非日常」的氛圍。

　　比起要與其周遭的自然或都市環境結合，宗教建築大部分時候更在意的是教義在三維空間中視覺化的回應與詮釋，此種視覺化型態漸漸成為一種具有意義的符號語彙——建築物件與建築量體本身同時成為宗教抽象概念的具象立體三維符號。

　　這就是為何當我們看見廟或教堂無論處於何種環境背景（都市或自然），都能如此容易地識別。我們看見的與其說這是宗教建築，不如說這是宗教符號。

去「常」以致「非常」

　　在建築類型上，佛寺、清真寺的設計、建造上與教堂有許多類似共通性，其中一個共同點是：過去這類建築傳統上會有某種程度的在一定範圍內去除日常的味道，適度的減少「生活味」，去「常」以致「非常」。

　　然而，這種「去生活味」在台灣的廟看不到，台灣的廟從過去到現在，都是極度世俗化的建築。各類柴米油鹽、衣食住行、男女老少的生活味爭先恐後的充斥在廟裡廟外，也許是供桌上的供品，也許是香爐的線香，也許是街頭巷尾形形色色的鄰里互動⋯⋯台灣的廟，將宗教的神聖與日常的世俗混合在一起的那部分，毫不忌諱、毫不掩飾地暴露出來。

　　這之間矛盾的是：表象上，大部分的廟在自然或都市環境中，在周邊的現代建築中，廟體建築本身都似乎張牙舞爪的與周邊格格不入，但在日常使用上與存在上卻又那麼理所當然：曲面屋頂上繁複到無以復加的裝飾，加裝了空氣濾淨設備的金爐，廟公的辦公桌或管理委員會辦公室內的泡茶桌⋯⋯理所當然地彷彿它們從未消失過，就像一直存在一般。

　　下面圖說僅對觀察記錄時針對廟的硬體做說明，這些廟所具備的符號（例如紅燈籠），帶領我們在都市中穿越水泥叢林中找到它們。

　　所謂
　　無所不在、
　　無神不拜、
　　無孔不入、
　　無奇不有，
　　可稱為寄生之廟。

　　但是，我們要如何認定具有這四「無」現象的空間是否為廟？對此，我們依其實體為判讀標準，即祭祀空間及相關物件的存在；而非基於其虛體，即宗教派別與祭祀行為的差異。

　　對寄生之廟的紀錄而言，有形空間的重要性更勝於無形的信仰。我們觀察、記錄的重點在於呈現其實體空間存在的現象，而非其信仰方面的需求。

　　以下僅就其空間組成討論。

Materialization of Religious Symbols

　　Religious buildings are materialization of religion on earth. They are the type of buildings that is of absolute specialization. Whether seen as a place or an object, they are buildings specialized by ideology, and often develop into a universal form, at least recognized and accepted by most believers. Besides, they traditionally create, more or less, a kind of heavenly atmosphere to weaken their mundanity and strengthen their spirituality.

　　Rather than fitting into the surroundings or urban environment, this type of buildings emphasizes receiving feedbacks on and interpretations of their three-dimensional visualization of doctrine. Their existence is a symbol, another three-dimensional sign of abstract religious concept. The architecture vocabulary and building volume together form symbols.

　　This is why when we see a temple or a church in a city or the countryside, we can always recognize it with ease. What we see is, rather than a religious building, more like a religious symbol.

De-mundan-ize to Heavenly

　　In architecture, temples share many qualities with mosques and churches. One thing in common is that they are all "demundanized" to a certain extent, in other words, to weaken their mundanity in order to demonstrate heavenly qualities.

　　However, this kind of demundanization is not seen in temples in Taiwan. On the contrary, temples in Taiwan have long been extremely mundane buildings, full of all kinds of living supplies, basic necessities of life, and people of all ages and both sexes. Offerings on the altar tables, incense sticks in the censers, and various neighborhood interactions on the streets are blatantly exposed in the temples as the sacredness of religion and mundanity on earth are mixed together.

　　It is so contradictory that surrounded by modern buildings in natural or urban areas, the construction of the temples seems flagrantly odd, yet their existence and usage are undoubtedly reasonable. The conspicuously ornamented curved rooftops, the censers equipped with air purifiers, and the desk of the temple abbot or the tea table in the management committee office, etc., are all taken for granted. They never disappear. It looks like they have always been there.

　　The captions below only explain the hardware recorded during observation. The symbols of these temples (e.g. red lanterns) lead us through the concrete jungle to the so-called parasitic temples, which are

　　ubiquitous
　　and polytheistic,
　　pervasive
　　and wondrous.

　　Nevertheless, how do we decide whether a place with the four qualities is a temple or not? To do it, we evaluate its physical part, the existence of a place of worship and its related objects, rather than its spiritual part, the difference of factions and rituals.

　　For WillipodiA, the physical space is more important than spiritual religion. Our observation report emphasizes presenting the fact of these temples' physical existence, not the religious needs they meet.

　　We will focus on their physical objects below.

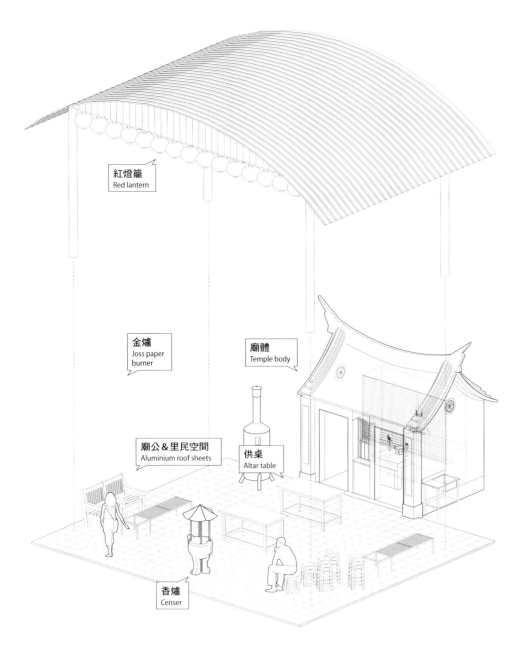

紅燈籠
Red lantern

金爐
Joss paper burner

廟體
Temple body

廟公＆里民空間
Aluminium roof sheets

供桌
Altar table

香爐
Censer

A 標配

廟體
供奉神明的實體空間。有些被自然環境圍塑而成，有些為人造的建築空間。

金爐
燃燒金紙的爐子。我們以放置金爐的位置，作為判定該寄生之廟是否具有侵占行為的主要依據。

香爐
插香的爐子，大多位於廟體之中。

B 選配

紅燈籠
傳統用來祈福的紅燈籠經常被廟宇所使用。有時藉由紅燈籠的掛放，我們得以辨識寄生之廟所延伸出的活動場所、廟埕與參拜路徑。

供桌
信眾擺放供品的空間物件，有些可被環境中自然形成的平台取代，如：石頭、分隔島等。

廟公＆里民空間（活動場所）
多數寄生之廟並不具備廟體之外的活動場所。其所能支配的空間越小，越顯得該廟的寄生程度、記錄價值越高。

A Standard equipment

Temple body
A physical space of worshiping deities. Some are surrounded by natural environment, others are within man-made buildings.

Joss paper burner
A device for burning joss paper. We judge a parasitic temple's parasitization on the location of the joss paper burner.

Censer
A container in which burning incense sticks are placed, mostly within the temple body.

B Optional equipment

Red lantern
Red lanterns for blessings by tradition are often used in temples. Sometimes through these red lanterns, we can recognize the venue or the square extended from a parasitic temple and its visiting route.

Altar table
An object on which worshippers place their offerings, sometimes replaced by natural platforms, like rocks, or even refuge islands.

Temple abbots' or residents' place
Most parasitic temples do not have venues other than the body. The less room a temple deploys, the higher its level of parasitization and value of documenting are.

欲望的有形面貌

　　書中的廟體本身，對我的意義不大，是它所處的「環境」吸引我的眼球，並賦予它在分類學上的意義。如果同樣的廟體被放置在別的地方，它就是一間再普通不過的廟。書中廟的命名大部分是來自它的環境，只有少數的暱稱來自廟本身。

　　理論上，這樣脫離日常與生活味的矛盾體是不會共存的，但台灣的廟卻恰恰提供這樣的共存空間，這樣的矛盾共存非但沒製造緊張，反而還能讓老一輩台灣人很放鬆，那並不單純只是宗教上的心靈寄託慰藉，也能讓身體放鬆。

　　羅馬人到處在羅馬的城市裡建鬥獸場與浴場，而台灣人則是在台灣城市裡到處建廟。

　　當欲望能以建築的形式呈現時，鬥獸場與浴場是那個時代羅馬人欲望的面貌；而廟是台灣人那個時代欲望的有形面貌。不管是精神需求與空間需求，這些成千成萬的廟背後代表的都是這件事：

　　「想要」！

資本轉換成宗教形式

　　台灣的民間資本，曾經風起雲湧，爭先恐後的向這樣的宗教建築高度集中。

　　在我們的祖父母輩之前，那個年代的善男信女把建廟當成財富儲存的一種形式，無限精神報酬的投資工具。

　　坦白說我真的很懷疑，以這樣子的集中程度而言：三步一小廟五步一大廟，廟幾乎無所不在，街頭巷尾都充斥著各類神明。照這資本密集的程度，會讓我們不禁懷疑曾經有過一段時間台灣最夯的職業就是建廟的師父。

　　許多廟尋求修建改建，
　　但因為本身從未取得合法建照，
　　始終處於曖昧鄉愿的地帶，
　　無法就地合法化，
　　必須取得建照之後才能夠進行改建。
　　所以只能持續這種狀態，
　　到自然破敗為止，
　　到自然死亡為止。

Tangible desires

The temple body in this book does not mean much to me. It is the environment in which the temple body is located that interests me and makes my taxonomy meaningful. If the same temple body is in another setting, it might become a completely normal temple. The naming of this book's temples mostly comes from their setting, and only few nicknames come from the temples themselves. In theory, such a contradictory entity so out of everyday life does not exist. However, Taiwan's temples provide exactly such space to embrace the contradiction without making it tense but soothing the elder generations in Taiwan. It is not only spiritual consolation in religion, but also relaxation in body.

While Romans built colosseums, thermae and balneae everywhere in Roman cities, the Taiwanese built temples around cities in Taiwan. Colosseums, thermae and balneae are reflection of the Roman lust at that time. When lust can be presented in architecture, the early Taiwanese demonstrated their lust through temples. Whether it is spiritual or spatial need, hundreds of thousands of temples represent their desire.

Capital transferred to religion

Taiwan's private capital was once frantically flooded to this kind of religious buildings. Worshippers of the era before our grandparents viewed building temples as a means of accumulating wealth, an investment instrument of unlimited spiritual rewards. Seeing that temples come in all sizes everywhere with myriad deities, I cannot help thinking such capital intensive mania once made temple construction workers the most in-demand job.

Many temples never acquire legal building permit. This ambiguous status becomes an obstacle when they seek renovation or reconstruction. Without planning permission, these temples can only maintain the status quo until they decay.

3

廟蒐集
Finding
the Temples

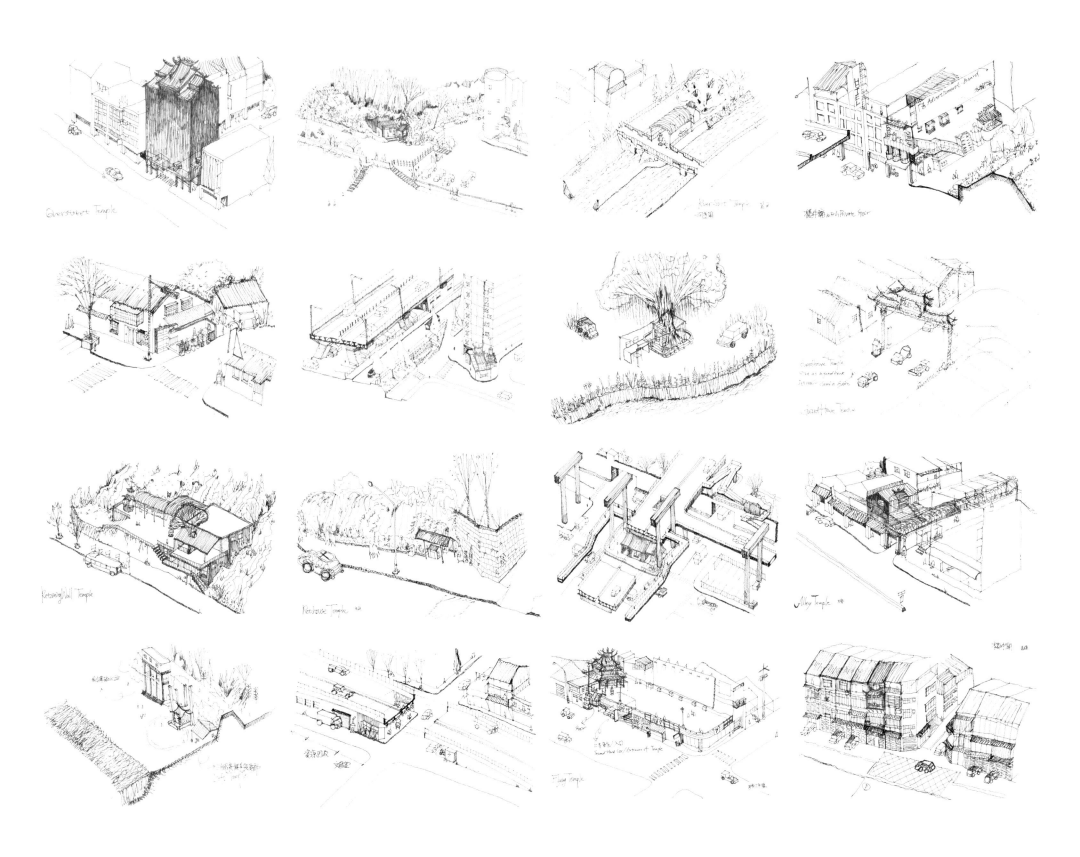

很多人最常問的問題是，我們究竟是如何找到這些廟的？這整個記錄過程所運用的方法，從傳統的田野調查到與時代結合的網路工具都有。而當我每次回答這問題時，我意識到：答案足以自成本書的一個章節。

A 搜索：

A1 傳統的田野調查肉搜（hunting）

第一步，最根本的方法無疑就是田野調查。

這些廟基本上大部分都是沒有大眾關注的無名之廟，所以，全部從網路上搜索的可能性極低。在寄生之廟記錄初期，畫定範圍的集體搜索與每個成員各自從自身居住周邊的鄰里開始，這兩種搜索方式已足夠幫助我們建立最基本，但不完整的分類表。

從每個成員各自住家周邊的鄰里開始，是最符合寄生之廟的出發點：觀察你身邊那些習以為常，卻自然而然被你忽略的事物與現象。

畫定範圍的集體搜索是既具有系統性，又同時具有參與者的隨機性：每個人隨機選擇的路線與認定有價值被記錄的隨機性。我們約定某時間一起自不同地方進入這個獵場獵廟，約定幾小時後於某處集合，分享討論彼此的戰果。其間透過手機通訊平台，如LINE，溝通並協調彼此的行動。

A2 獵廟地圖先於現場探勘

藉助搜尋Web資訊預覽，如Google Earth, Google Maps, Google Street View 等，再經查詢民政局網站，我們在出發獵廟前，就已經能定位獵物的位置，並且搭配寄生之廟初期建立的最基本分類表，預先判斷出有價值的獵物。這點大大地節省了地毯式搜索的時間，同時也擴大了搜索範圍，獵廟的獵場範圍比原本的田野調查大上好幾倍，有助於找到未發現的新品種。

B 成果整合平台：

B1 跨時間與空間的田野調查

當獵場因LINE與Goolgle Earth的協調作業擴大後，大家的搜索行動不再同時而採分區進行，只需要選擇自己想去的區域搜索。事實上，搜索後期的新廟往往靠大家在獵場範圍外，平時因旅遊或在城市間移動中找到，上傳至LINE和雲端。

B2 群組的同步協作

這個搜索組織事實上不存在，成員彼此不認識。但透過同一個LINE群組將這群人聚在一起，在不同時間不同地點有共同的目標，或者說有共同的消遣，做同一件事的同步協作。

C 工具：

運用傳統與當代工具，從拍照、手繪、建模，到影像軟體。對於發現有記錄價值的寄生之廟，會先以拍照與手繪呈現，再與WillipodiA成員討論過，對照分類表上所需要的廟後，才決定哪些寄生之廟能夠獲選進入建3D模型階段。此外，YouBike的出現，讓獵廟者的搜索範圍變大。空拍攝影的出現，在非禁航區範圍內，能使照片更具軸測視野。

D 記錄圖面：參考Real-time即時界面

即時戰略遊戲（Real-time strategy）在我所屬的遊戲世代中橫空出世，有別於過去傳統回合制（turn-based）的遊戲，即時制的遊戲中，時間是真實的時間，時間是一分一秒在流逝的，這迥異於回合制的兵棋操作，每步下手前的時間是凍結的，坦白說，每步下手後的時間也還是凍結的，因為這還是屬於舊時代舊思維的靜態對弈遊戲，搭載在新時代的新平台上。

直到即時制遊戲的出現，除了真正發揮PC時代電腦主機才能有的強大多工運算能力，它真正改變人手腦並用時，其對應電腦的界面關係：動態遊戲的界面設計代表了人在面對真實時間的分秒必爭下，所能處理的資訊量的上限，下判斷時需要知道的資訊量，以及所能做出的反應動作。

多要多到你能充分掌握大局，同時少要少到你不用手忙腳亂。

致我所屬的時代
致這些偉大的界面設計者
寄生之廟的記錄圖面比照這些界面設計而成

E 資訊儲存方式

在我的想像中，保存這些成果的最終方式並不只是書，書只是現階段。可超越書的局限性，更理想的保存方式是GIS地理資訊系統（Geographic Information System）。前段研究過程中，我們雖大量使用Google Maps來標記廟的位置，但後來我才想通對於後段的記錄成果，也可以用類似的方法來保存。甚至將其轉化成手機遊戲也是一種可能，我相信寄生之廟到下個階段時，應該會出現更進步、更有趣、更能回應時代性並呈現這個觀察紀錄的載體。

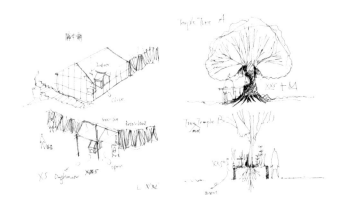

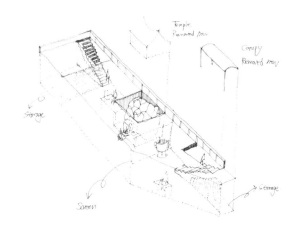

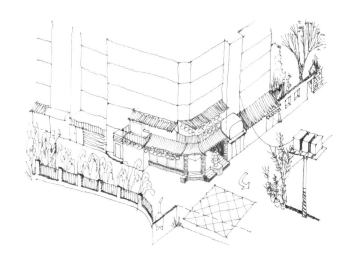

A lot of people are wondering how we find these temples. Both traditional field research and the latest internet tools come in handy. When I try to answer this question, I realize that it can be a whole chapter of the book.

A Searching

A1 Conventional field research — hunting

Our first step is undoubtedly the basic method, field research. Since these temples are mostly unknown to the public, it is not likely to find them all on the internet. We started by observing our own neighborhood individually and assigning a range to conduct a search in groups. In the early stages, the results provided an incomplete but basic taxonomy chart.

The first way, observing one's own neighborhood, is exactly what drove us to do the study: to pay attention to what we are used to and ignore around us.

The second way, conducting a group field research within a designated region, is both systematic and random because each member selected the route randomly and the chance of a temple to be regarded as record-worthy is random, too. We entered the region through different accesses at the same time, and coordinated our operation through mobile messaging apps like LINE. In a couple of hours, we met up somewhere to share and discuss our observation.

A2 Online maps before on-site jobs

After using Google Earth, Google Maps, and Google Street View with websites of the civil affairs, we could locate the targets in advance and evaluate them according to our rudimentary taxonomy. This greatly saved our time of conducting a blanket search and widens the range to many times bigger than that of a field research, helping us discover new breeds.

B Result integration platform

B1 An unconventional field research with no time and space limitations

Our search operations no longer needed to be synchronized, thanks to LINE and Google Earth, which facilitated our coordination. After the scope was widened and divided, we simply chose the regions we liked. In fact, during the last stages, discovery of new targets was often made outside the designated range but on the way of a journey or when moving between cities, and then shared in LINE or uploaded to the cloud.

B2 Group coordination

Technically this search organization does not exist. The members do not know each other, but get together in a LINE group at different time, in different places, with the same goal or recreation, and in collaboration with each other to complete a task.

C Tools:

We use both traditional and modern tools, including photography, freehand drawing, modeling and image processing. When a parasitic temple worthy of recording pops up, we take or draw a picture of it first. After discussing with Willipodia members and checking our taxonomy chart, we will decide whether the temple can move on to the stage of 3D modeling. Besides, the introduction of YouBike widens our search range, and the application of aerial photography outside the no-fly zones provides an even more complete view.

D Graphics: Real-time interface

Real-time strategy (RTS) burst into my era. Unlike traditional turn-based games where the game progresses incrementally in turns, players of real-time strategy make their moves simultaneously while the time in the game ticks away as it does in reality. It was not until the introduction of RTS did the powerful multitasking capability of personal computers got fully utilized. It totally changed the interface which people used to control computers. The design of RTS tests the maximum load of data people can handle, the amount of information needed to make decisions, and the response they are able to make under the time pressure.

It must be plenty enough for you to see the big picture, yet not too much so you can handle it in an orderly fashion.

To the era I belong to.
To those great interface designers.
The graphics of parasitic temples are here because of those epoch-making creations.

E Data storage

In my dreams, the results of my study do not just go into books. Printing is just for now, and my ideal way to preserve them is through a geographic information system (GIS), which breaks the limitations of books. In the early stages of our research, we used Google Maps a lot to label the temples. It was not until later did it struck me that I could make use of something similar for data storage, or even transformed it into a mobile game. I believe that at the next stage of parasitic temple research, there will be more advanced, more interesting, and more suitable method to present our documentary.

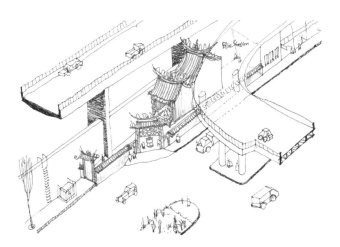

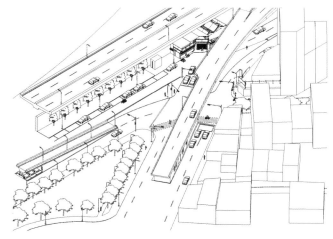

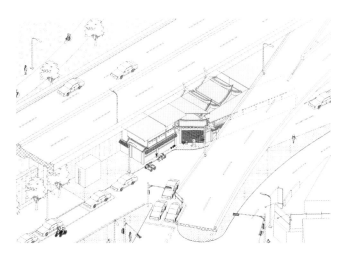

4

廟屬性
Temple Attributes

記錄這些廟的同時也記錄都市紋理與居民生活型態，都市變遷的活化石，廟宇周邊就是都市的縮影，都市的切片，我們只是選擇廟作為拓印城市的媒介。

在記錄的過程中，除了拓印其周邊肉眼所能看見「物相之內」的實體空間；在「物相之外」還需要同時發展另一套代表廟「屬性」的符號，和記錄物相的照片與等角圖相同，都是用來說明廟的各種面向的圖素，濃縮了看得見與看不見的部分、不同廟之間的個體異同。

這套符號的建立，除了更深一層次的記錄廟外，也幫助我們更清楚地梳理下一章節會談到的廟的分類。

屬性由廟的「天性」與「個性」構成

廟的「天性」與廟的分類有直接的關係，決定了廟的種類：

- 生於都市形成之前／生於都市形成之後
- 自然宿主／人造宿主
- 建築內寄生／建築外寄生

「個性」與廟的分類無關，所代表的僅是該廟案例本身的個體差異：

- 基地：天／地／山／水
- 廟埕完整性
- 侵占行為
- 大小
- 中式屋頂
- 廟公空間
- 一神多神
- 看不見的廟
- 多重寄生
- 廟中廟
- 垂直移動／水平移動
- 構造與材質

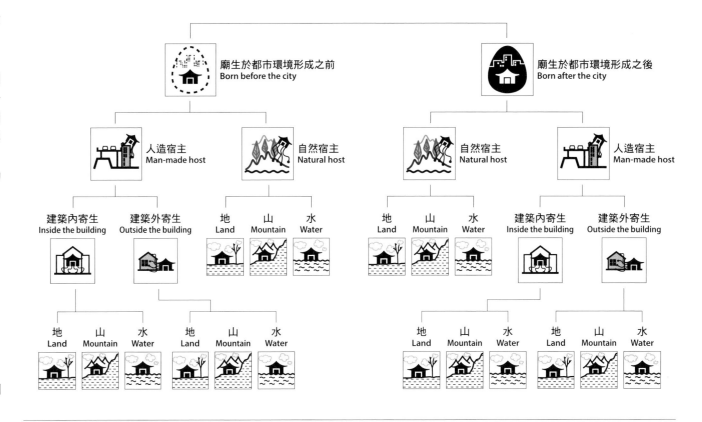

Documenting these temples is also documenting the fabric of cities and urban lifestyles. It is a living fossil of urban changes. The surroundings of temples are the epitome, the biopsy of a city. We just choose temples as the medium to make a rubbing of the city.

During the process, we have to not only record what we see in reality with pictures and isometric graphs, but also develop another set of labels to help us distinguish the difference among temples. These labels provide a more thorough record of the temples, and aid us in clarifying the taxonomy of temples in the next chapter.

The attributes of temples consist of dispositions and characters

Dispositions are directly related to the classification of a temple, determining its category.

- Built before/after the formation of the city
- Natural/Man-made host
- Parasitizing inside/outside the building

Characters are not about the classification of a temple, but show only its individual differences.

- Base: sky/land/mountain/water
- The completeness of the temple square
- Invasion
- Size
- Chinese-style rooftops
- Office of the temple abbot
- Single deity or multiple deities
- Invisible temple
- Multiple parasitic
- Double layered
- Vertical/Horizontal movement
- Structure and material

廟的生成時間

廟生於都市環境形成之前：
　　如圓環廟，分隔島廟存在於都市道路建造前。
廟生於都市環境形成之後：
　　如街屋廟、垂直廟存在於都市成形之後。
　　所謂的現代都市環境，不再因人類聚落而形成，反而因
　　汽車的交通行為、各項基礎建設而形成。都市從原本以
　　人為主的尺度轉變成以車為主的尺度，樓與樓的距離也
　　被車道寬窄定義。

Building a temple

The temple was built before the formation of the city, like the round-about temple or the traffic island temple, both of which were built before the urban roads came into existence.
The temple was built after the formation of the city, like the street house temple or vertical temple, both of which were built after the city had been formed.
The so-called urban environment is not about human settlement but the use of automobiles and establishment of infrastructure. Measurements in a city used to be based on the residents, but now they are based on cars. The distance between buildings is defined by the width of roads.

自然／人造宿主

自然宿主：
　　廟宇本身棲息於自然元素，如樹中或岩中。
人造宿主：
　　廟宇本身棲息於人造物，如建築物或基礎工程構造等。

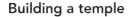

Natural/Man-made host

Natural host:
　　The temple takes natural elements like trees or rocks as its host.
Man-made host:
　　The temple takes man-made objects like buildings or fundamental facilities as its host.

建築內／外寄生

建築內寄生：

　　廟是設置於既有的建築物裡面，不過通常會在建築立面上表現寺廟語彙，以利辨認，但外觀主體仍是原建築。

建築外寄生：

　　廟是在寄生在既有的建築物外面，如屋頂廟。

Parasitizing inside/outside the building

Parasitizing inside the building:

　　The temple is inside an existing building, usually with some religious signatures on the façade for recognition, but the original building can still be made out.

Parasitizing outside the building:

　　The temple is outside an existing building, like the rooftop temple.

基地：天／地／山／水

廟依所處的基地屬性分為：

- 天：本體離地於空中，立基在高於都市地面層之上的建築裡面或上面，如樓中廟、空中廟、屋頂廟等。
- 地：本體落地於都市地面層，大部分的廟都是，如一樓改造廟、畸零地廟、街屋廟、垂直廟等。
- 山：本體近山坡地，如石中廟、坡腳廟、擋土牆廟等。
- 水：本體近水域，如水中廟、河岸廟、河道廟等。

Base: sky/land/mountain/water

The attributes of the base of a temple are:

- Sky: the temple body is based in the air above the urban ground level, like in-between temples, flying temples, and rooftop temples.
- Land: the temple body is based on the urban ground level (and most of the temples do), like first-floor-modified temples, fraction temples, street house temples, and vertical temples.
- Mountain: The temple body is based near the hillside, like rock temples, footslope temples, and retaining wall temples.
- Water: The temple body is based near water, like water temples, riverbank temples, and waterway temples.

廟埕完整性

許多寄生於都市夾縫與邊緣的無名小廟，沒有完整廟埕，
如一樓改造廟、樓中廟、分離廟等。

The completeness of the temple square

Many nameless temples parasitizing in the urban gaps or
boarders do not have a complete square, like first-floor-modified
temples, in-between temples, and separate temples.

侵占行為

許多沒有完整廟埕的廟會直接使用入口處的都市空間作
為廟埕延伸，侵占形式有多種，可能侵占道路、人行道、
騎樓、屋頂露臺等。

Invasion

Many temples without a complete square extend their territory
at their entrance. This kind of invasion can happen in many
places, like the road, the sidewalk, the qilou, or the roof terrace.

中式屋頂

與民眾情感、認知、意識形態難以割捨的中式屋頂，至今仍為廟此一宗教建築形式選擇上的主流。

Chinese-style rooftop

The Chinese-style rooftop, which are deeply connected with people's feelings, cognition, and ideology, is still the mainstream when it comes to building a temple.

廟公空間

通常廟都會有看管廟的管理員，但許多寄生之廟小到無法提供廟公的辦公空間，或是雖有，卻克難到不可思議。

Office of the temple abbot

Usually there is an abbot in charge of a temple, but many parasitic temples are so small that they can only provide their abbots with either tiny space or even nothing at all.

一神／多神

台灣是一個宗教多神多元，信仰包容度很大的地方，你可以發現很多廟中不只供奉一個神祇，可以一個主神搭配別的神明。

Single deity or multiple deities

Taiwan is very tolerant and inclusive in terms of religion. You can find many temples enshrine more than one deity. It seems that those deities do not mind having company.

看不見的廟

廟在都市中的寄生現象演化至今，某些類型已逐漸脫離民眾認知中傳統廟所具備的建築語彙所構成的形象，其中具備廟的功能，卻無廟的傳統外形者，是謂「看不見的廟」。

Invisible temple

The phenomenon of parasitic temples in urban areas has evolved to the extent that some types have no longer had the signature of traditional temples with which the public are familiar – that is, they serve the function of a temple, but are not built with traditional exterior design. This is the so-called invisible temples.

多重寄生

具備兩個以上寄主的廟即具備多元寄生能力，在廟的命名上以主觀上較顯著或確實較主要的宿主命名。

Multiple parasitic

Multiple parasitic temples take more than one hosts. When it comes to naming, the one that is more conspicuous or more dominant will be considered first.

廟中廟

有些廟在演化的過程中，會在廟本體之外增加通常是鋼構鐵皮造的屋頂；蓋過原來的廟體，有時會圍塑出有遮蔭的廟埕。

Double layered

Some temples, during evolution, will acquire certain add-ons, usually a metal roof, which covers the whole temple body and sometime even provides the shade to the temple square.

移動能力

有些廟具備移動能力，像一個移動攤車或被臨時安放在卡車或船上。有些廟甚至在漲潮時，可以將整個廟體往上抬升。

Vertical/Horizontal movement

Some temples can move, for example, a vendor cart temple or a temple temporarily located on a pickup truck or a boat. There is even a temple that can lift itself when the tide is in.

構造與材質

目前的調查區分出三種造廟技術工法：
1. 磚木石造；
2. 混凝土磁磚；
3. 鋼構鐵皮。

Structure and material

So far there are three construction methods of temples in Taiwan:
1. Brick, wood, and stone.
2. Concrete and tiles.
3. Steel structure with iron plates.

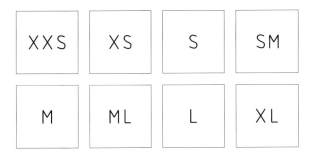

XXS	XS	S	SM
M	ML	L	XL

大小

本書收錄大多廟的尺寸都不會太大，區分為XXS、XS、S、M、L、XL，介於兩種尺寸之間的，則以SM、ML標示。本書沒有收錄在中國或台灣建築史上能列入XXXL級的模範大廟。

Size

Most of the temples in this book are not big. They are categorized into XXS, XS, S, M, and L. This book does not include the XXXL temples in the history of architecture in China or Taiwan.

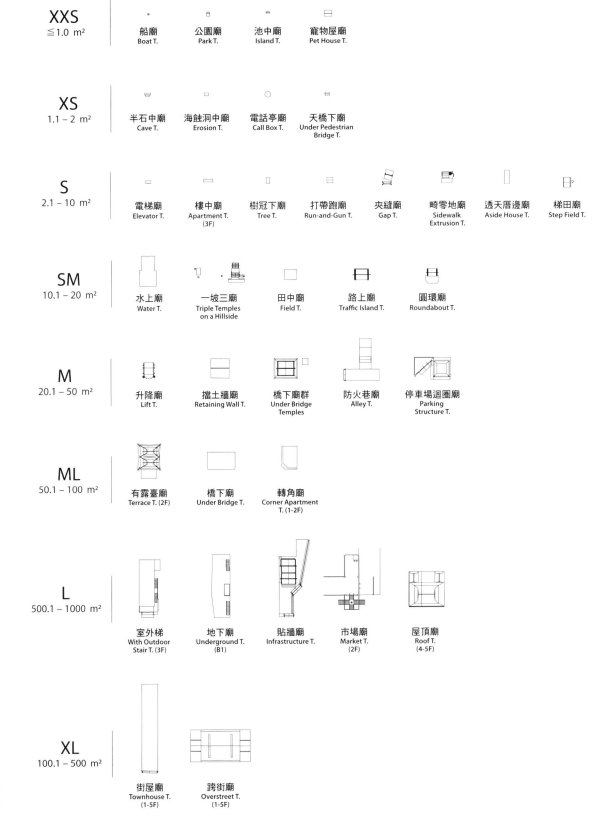

XXS ≦1.0 m²
船廟 Boat T. — 公園廟 Park T. — 池中廟 Island T. — 寵物屋廟 Pet House T.

XS 1.1 – 2 m²
半石中廟 Cave T. — 海蝕洞中廟 Erosion T. — 電話亭廟 Call Box T. — 天橋下廟 Under Pedestrian Bridge T.

S 2.1 – 10 m²
電梯廟 Elevator T. — 樓中廟 Apartment T. (3F) — 樹冠下廟 Tree T. — 打帶跑廟 Run-and-Gun T. — 夾縫廟 Gap T. — 畸零地廟 Sidewalk Extrusion T. — 透天厝邊廟 Aside House T. — 梯田廟 Step Field T.

SM 10.1 – 20 m²
水上廟 Water T. — 一坡三廟 Triple Temples on a Hillside — 田中廟 Field T. — 路上廟 Traffic Island T. — 圓環廟 Roundabout T.

M 20.1 – 50 m²
升降廟 Lift T. — 擋土牆廟 Retaining Wall T. — 橋下廟群 Under Bridge Temples — 防火巷廟 Alley T. — 停車場迴圈廟 Parking Structure T.

ML 50.1 – 100 m²
有露臺廟 Terrace T. (2F) — 橋下廟 Under Bridge T. — 轉角廟 Corner Apartment T. (1-2F)

L 500.1 – 1000 m²
室外梯 With Outdoor Stair T. (3F) — 地下廟 Underground T. (B1) — 貼牆廟 Infrastructure T. — 市場廟 Market T. (2F) — 屋頂廟 Roof T. (4-5F)

XL 100.1 – 500 m²
街屋廟 Townhouse T. (1-5F) — 跨街廟 Overstreet T. (1-5F)

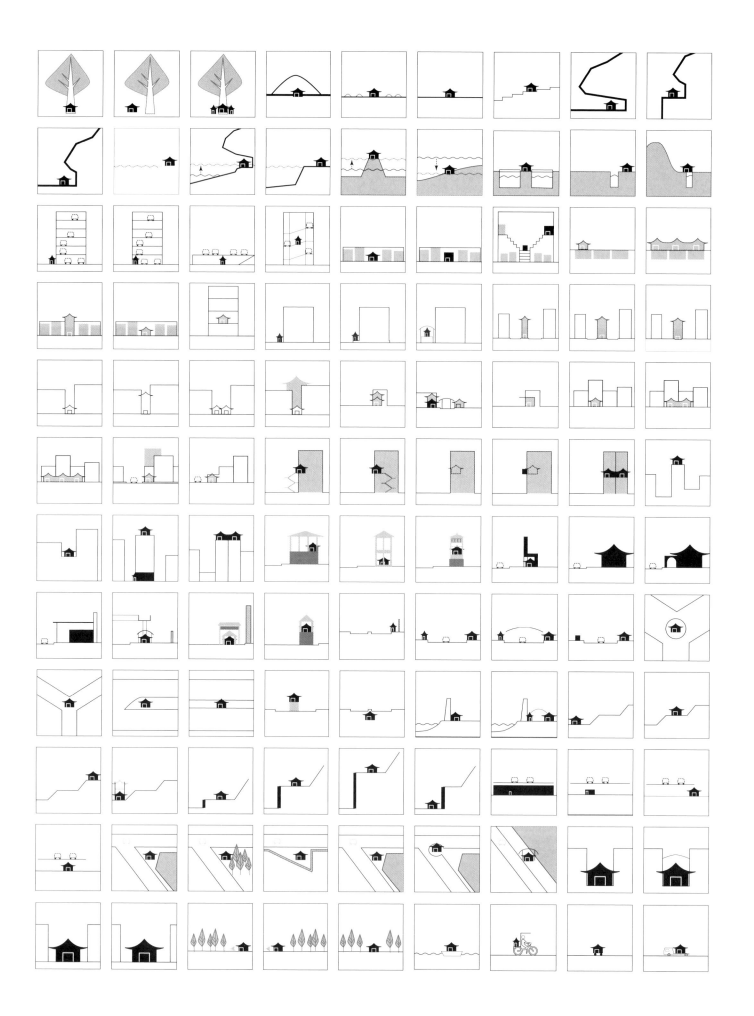

5

廟分類
Temple Taxonomies

這些廟，寄生在都市之中。
這些廟，不是想像，
而是在台灣都市的水泥叢林中
如生物般自然生長、自然演化而來。

WillipodiA團隊嘗試將在台灣四處網羅、蒐集、觀察、記錄而來的廟——如寄生的生物一般的寄生之廟，進行如生物分類般的分類。

　　既謂寄生，即必有宿主。

　　我們據寄生之廟與宿主（環境）的關係，依其所寄生的宿主性質及寄生方式，進行都市與建築類型學上的分類，好比生物分類學的界、門、綱、目、科、屬、種，WillipodiA團隊建立了域、界、族、系、支、子分類的系統。

　　藉由整理蒐羅而來的廟，反映出台灣都市生活中隨處可見的日常現象。下頁以分類系統表初步說明整個分類架構。

These temples parasitize in the cities.
They are not imaginary,
but like living creatures growing and evolving
in the concrete jungles in Taiwan.

WillipodiA tries to define and name groups of parasitic temples which are searched, observed, and documented throughout Taiwan, just like what biologists do to animals and plants.

　　Where there are parasites, there are hosts.

　　Based on the relationship between parasitic temples and their hosts (the environment), the qualities of the hosts and the way of parasitizing, we define and group parasitic temples in architecture. Just like kingdom, phylum, class, order, family, genus, and species in biology, WillipodiA also proposed a scheme of classification: domain, kingdom, tribe, clan, family, and branch.

　　The temples we documented reflect everyday lives around the cities in Taiwan. The following explains the whole taxonomy of parasitic temples.

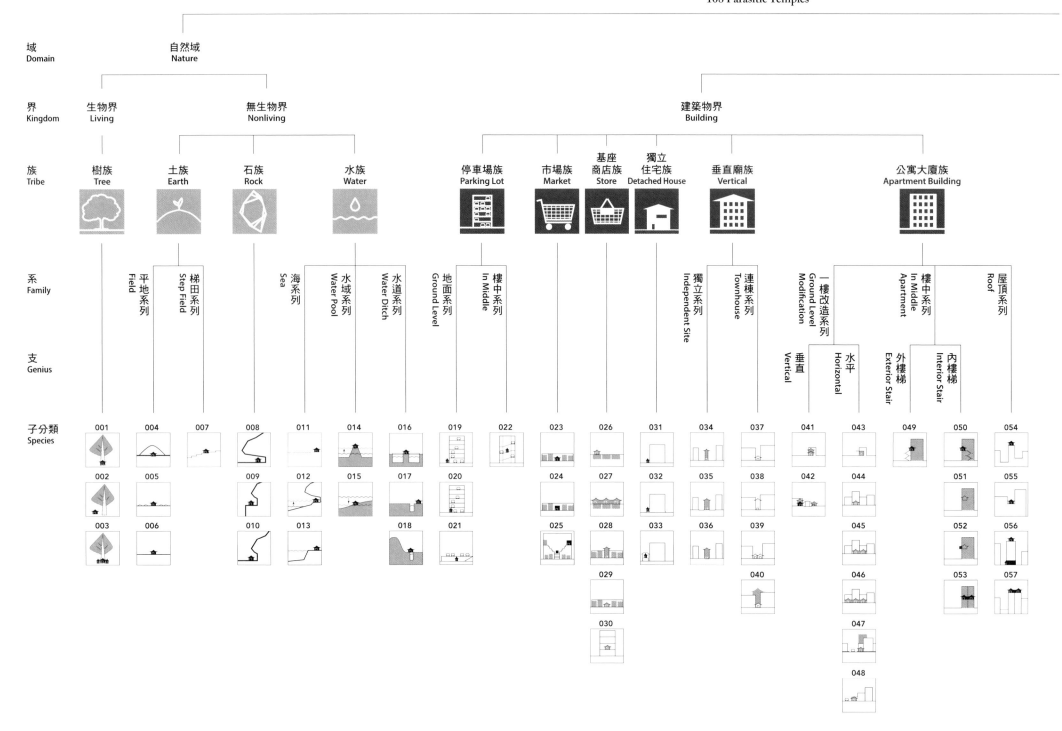

一〇八種寄生之廟
108 Parasitic Temples

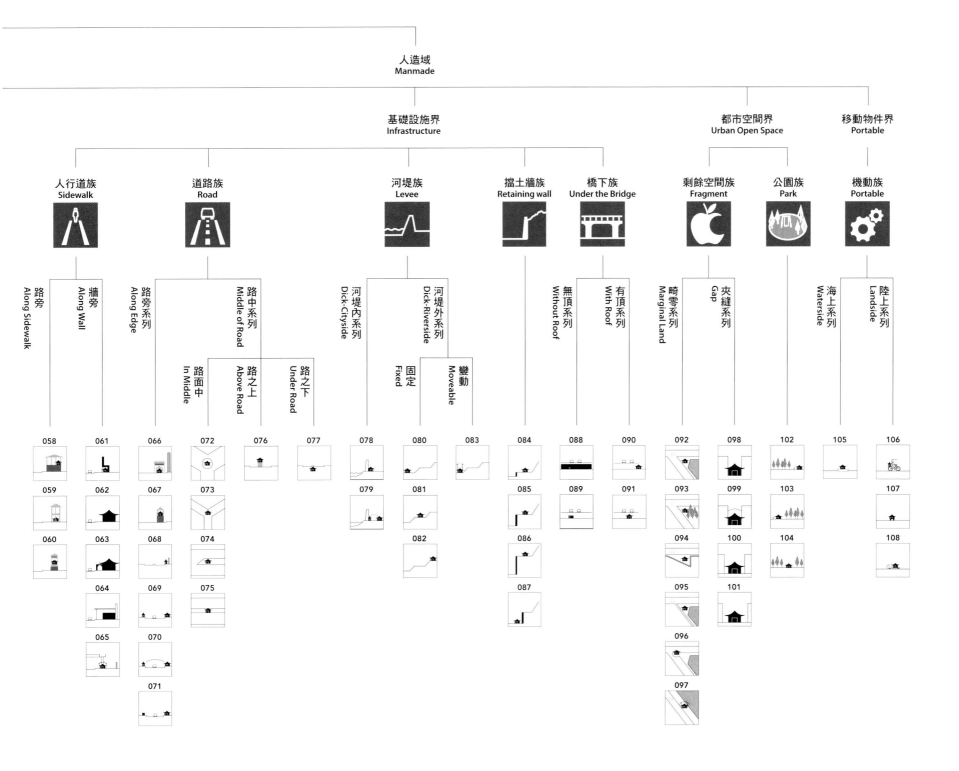

域　依照宿主性質，區分成自然與人造兩種主要類別。域之分野，與都市環境形成的前後有所關連：以自然界物件為宿主的廟多半生於都市環境形成之前，而以人造物為宿主的廟則在都市環境形成前後都有可能。

界　存在於人造物前的自然萬物，依其本身是否具生物性進行分類，能被區分成生物界以及無生物界兩大類別。

現代都市環境的人造物種類包羅萬象，我們將有寄生之廟存在的人造物進行初步分類：從實體的基礎設施及建築物，乃至虛體的都市開放空間，甚至是穿梭其中的移動物件，都能見到它的蹤跡。

族　由各界向下細分成18族。分到這層時，寄生之廟的各式各樣的宿主們已能被明確的辨認出來。蒐集而來的寄生之廟，都能在這層的分類系統下找到它的歸屬。我們相信我們已將台灣四處無處不見的各類寄生之廟納入這層分類系統中。

Domain　According to the qualities of the host, domains are grouped in two: nature and man-made. The classification of domain is related to the time of urban formation. Temples taking nature objects as hosts were mostly built before the city is formed, while temples taking man-made objects as hosts were built either before or after the formation of the city.

Kingdom　All nature things, other than man-made, can be grouped into living or nonliving according to whether they have life.
In modern urban environment, there is a variety of man-made objects. We roughly group them into tangible infrastructure and building, intangible urban open space, and even mobile objects moving through the city.

Tribe　The four kingdoms are further divided into eighteen tribes. At this ranking, various hosts of parasitic temples can be clearly identified. All documented parasitic temples belong to a certain tribe. We believe that this classification is complete enough to cover all kinds of parasitic temples in Taiwan.

自然域
Nature

　生物界
　Living

　無生物界
　Nonliving

人造域
Manmade

　建築物界
　Building

　基礎設施界
　Infrastructure

　都市空間界
　Urban Open Space

　移動物件界
　Portable

生物，尤其是植物，生長並記錄時間。聚落中的大樹能遮蔭避雨，往往能成為村落中居民交流聚集處，也成了廟寄生的所在。

Living creatures, especially plants, grow and record time. Big trees in a settlement provide the shade and shelter and often become a place where residents gather together – that is, where a parasitic temple finds its host.

自然萬物比人類存在的時間更為久遠。廟宇最早就寄生在這些或立地特殊的土、石；或與生存相關的必要自然元素土、水之中；表現出與其親近／崇敬的關係。

Natural things exist on earth much longer than human beings. In early times, temples resided on special rocks or in necessary elements of life like earth and water to show their close and reverential relationship.

為了現代都市人生活而出現的各類建築，在都市生活中仍有對信仰的需求與渴望而被設立於建築中的廟，無論是出現在建築物的內外，都可視為是一種建築物的複合使用模式，且多半出現於建築物完成後。這族系即是所謂生於都市之後的寄生之廟。

All kinds of buildings are constructed to meet people's need in modern cities. In urban life, however, the need for belief still exists, and drives people to set up temples inside or outside the buildings. This can be seen as a complex, and often appear after the building is finished. Therefore, it is the so-called parasitic temples born after urban formation.

為了現代都市網絡運作而存在的各類基礎設施在今天成為寄生之廟的棲地。或許在這些基礎設施出現前，這些基地就已經是廟的棲地，因為基礎設施的興建而成為了寄生之廟，是一種就地合法的鄉愿與妥協。這族系即是所謂生於都市之前的寄生之廟。

Infrastructure facilities, which are built to facilitate operation of a city, also become hosts to parasitic temples today. These temples came into existence before the facilities were built, and their construction made them parasitic temples, which is a compromise between the government and the locals. Therefore, it is the so-called parasitic temples born before urban formation.

現代都市「圖形背景實虛關係」中的開放虛空間，基於信仰的需求也出現了占領和寄生的族系紀錄。其中包括寄生於都市中畸零、剩餘空地的剩餘空間族；以及恰好與這族非常對比的，寄生於都市中完整的、被妥善規劃的公園等開放空間的公園族。

In modern cities, some open space is being occupied by parasitic temples due to the need of belief. Some temples find hosts in scattered, fragmented space, while others do so in well-designed parks with plenty of comfortable room.

都市中，人造物件除了固定不動的實體和虛體外，也有大量帶領人移動、穿梭其間的移動工具。對於信仰需求的欲望也在這樣的空間中具體呈現，同時帶有一些臨時性、宣傳或祭典節慶般的性質存在。

機動族包含在陸上的三輪車廟、攤車廟、卡車廟，以及位於水上的船廟。或許未來能發現在熱氣球上的「空中」系。

Other than tangible and intangible urban man-made objects, there are also a lot of means of transportation by which people can move between places. The need of belief can also be presented in this kind of space with qualities of temporariness, advertisement, or festivity.
The mobile tribe includes tricycle temples, vendor cart temples, pickup truck temples on the land, and boat temples in the water. Maybe there will hot air balloon temples in the sky.

「前人種樹，後人乘涼」、「十年樹木」，樹在文化中總有種時間的延續性。大樹本身在早期的聚落中提供了戶外的遮蔭，往往成了人群聚集的公共場所，看著後浪推前浪，看著聚落興衰。廟宇也因這樣的特性寄生其中。

In Chinese, we have many proverbs about trees, like "Someone is sitting in the shade today because someone planted a tree a long time ago," or "It takes ten years to grow trees." Trees imply continuity of time in many cultures. They provide the shade and often become a place where people gather together. They watch the ups and downs of a village, and for that temples tend to take them as hosts.

自然域｜生物界
Domain: **Nature**
Kingdom: **Living**

樹族
Tribe: **TREE**

001
樹幹中
In Stem

002 → 案例 1 *
樹冠下
Under Crown

003
一樹三廟
Tripple in Tree

土是早期農耕社會中，孕育出各種作物的基本元素。早期的寄生之廟，便寄生在這因為地形形態略異的自然場域中。

In early agricultural societies, the earth grew all kinds of crops. Parasitic temples then would find their hosts in various natural landscapes.

自然域｜無生物界
Domain: **Nature**
Kingdom: **Nonliving**

土族
Tribe: **EARTH**

平地系列
Field

梯田系列
Step Field

004
墳包
In Soil

005
鹽田
Salt Pan

006 → 案例 2
田
Field

007 → 案例 3
梯田
Step Field

山中巨石形成的岩洞或凹縫，成為了來往的旅人或是地方居民經過、暫歇停留的地點。廟就在這天險或是天然避雨處寄生。

The caves or gaps formed by rocks in the mountains become rest stops for travelers or passing locals. Temples find hosts in this kind of natural barriers or shelters.

自然域｜無生物界
Domain: **Nature**
Kingdom: **Nonliving**

石族
Tribe: **ROCK**

008
全在石中
All in Rock

009
岩壁中
In the Cliff

010 → 案例 4
半在石中
Half in rock

＊ → 案例 1，即代表參見 Chapter 6 案例 1 頁面

聚落常依水而生。大海、湖泊、埤塘、灌溉水道、水溝各類相異的水族旁都有廟宇寄生的蹤跡。

Settlements are often founded near water. Parasitic temples can be found near the sea, the lake, the pond, the irrigation waterway or even the ditch.

自然域｜無生物界
Domain: **Nature**
Kingdom: **Nonliving**

水族
Tribe: **WATER**

海系列
Sea

011
沙灘上
Sandy Coast

012→ 案例 5
海蝕洞中
In the Sea Caves

013
岩岸上
Rocky Coast

水域系列
Water Pool

014→ 案例 6
池中
In the Middle

015
水下
Under Water

水道系列
Water Ditch

016→ 案例 7
水上
Above Water

017
水邊
Aside Water

018
水溝
Across Water

都市演化到以車行為主的時代之後，停車場成了都市中必備的建築或空間。

After automobiles dominate the urban traffic, parking lots become a necessity in the city.

人造域｜建築物界
Domain: **Manmade**
Kingdom: **Building**

停車場族
Tribe: **PARKING LOT**

地面系列
Ground Level

019
停車場外
Outside of the Building

020→ 案例 8
停車場內
Within the Building

021
一樓頂停車場
Under Parking

樓中系列
In Middle

022→ 案例 9
斜坡道中
In the Center of Circular Ramp

都市聚落中，人群聚集交流買賣的地方形成了市場。早期或近代的市場中往往能發現寄生廟的存在。

In urban areas, the place where people gather to trade becomes a market, and parasitic temples are often found in early or recent markets.

人造域｜建築物界
Domain: **Manmade**
Kingdom: **Building**

市場族
Tribe: **MARKET**

023
市場內有頂
In Market with Roof

024
市場內無頂
In Market without Roof as a Unit in the Market

025→ 案例 10
市場內樓中
In Market

民間私人設立的店鋪，也有寄生廟的蹤跡。但究竟是先有店才有廟，還是先有廟才有店，就因每個寄生廟的不同而有差異了。

Many private stores also have trace of parasitic temples. But whether the store or the temple comes first, it varies in every situation.

人造域｜建築物界
Domain: **Manmade**
Kingdom: **Building**

基座商店族
Tribe: **STORE**

026 → 案例 11
有露臺
Above Shops with
a Big Platform

027
無露臺
Above Shops
without a Platform

028
商店上
Above Shops

029
餐廳
In Restaurant

030
百貨公司
In Department Store

私人的獨立住宅旁，往往能發現較不正式的、小型的、型態各異的寄生廟的蹤跡。

Around private detached houses, there are often some less formal, tiny, and peculiar parasitic temples

人造域｜建築物界
Domain: **Manmade**
Kingdom: **Building**

獨立住宅族
Tribe: **DETACHED HOUSE**

031 → 案例 12
透天厝邊地
Aside House

032
防潮箱
Dry Box

033
防潮箱有頂
Dry Box with Canopy

隨著現代都市的發展，建築越蓋越高；寄生廟也在社會變遷的過程隨之更新，垂直發展。

With the development of modern cities, buildings become taller and taller. Parasitic temples also follow the trend to grow vertically.

人造域｜建築物界
Domain: **Manmade**
Kingdom: **Building**

垂直廟族
Tribe: **VERTICAL**

獨立系列
Independent Site

034
窄
Skinny

035
典型
Typical

036 → 案例 13
跨街
Overstreet

連棟系列
Townhouse

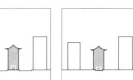

037
單一
Single

038 → 案例 14
單一且高
Single Tall

039
雙併
Double

040
大廟在街屋後
Big temple inside
after townhouse

公寓大廈是現代都市多數人棲居，且活動時間長的生活空間。此族有著我們所記錄的類別中最豐富多樣的寄生廟類型，分成三系列：一樓改造、樓中、屋頂。

Most urban residents live in apartment buildings and spent a lot of time there. In this category, we documented the most diverse parasitic temples: first-floor-modified, in-between, and rooftop.

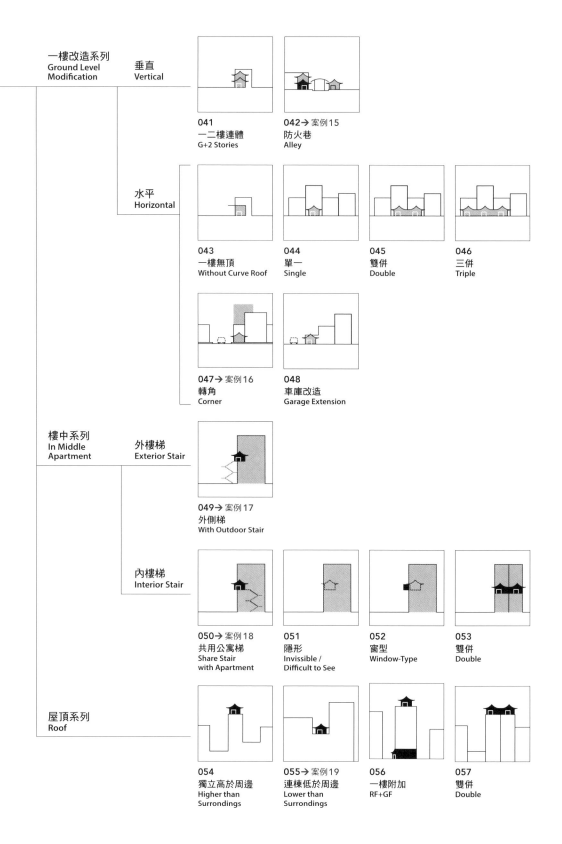

 人造域｜建築物界
Domain: Manmade
Kingdom: Building

公寓大廈族
Tribe: **APARTMENT BUILDING**

一樓改造系列
Ground Level Modification

垂直 Vertical

041
一二樓連體
G+2 Stories

042→案例15
防火巷
Alley

水平
Horizontal

043
一樓無頂
Without Curve Roof

044
單一
Single

045
雙併
Double

046
三併
Triple

047→案例16
轉角
Corner

048
車庫改造
Garage Extension

樓中系列
In Middle Apartment

外樓梯
Exterior Stair

049→案例17
外側梯
With Outdoor Stair

內樓梯
Interior Stair

050→案例18
共用公寓梯
Share Stair with Apartment

051
隱形
Invissible / Difficult to See

052
窗型
Window-Type

053
雙併
Double

屋頂系列
Roof

054
獨立高於周邊
Higher than Surrondings

055→案例19
連棟低於周邊
Lower than Surrondings

056
一樓附加
RF+GF

057
雙併
Double

人行道是都市空間中，人在建築間移動行走的通道。除了街道和路樹外，也有寄生之廟在其上。人行道和寄生廟的先後關係大多先有廟，而後才有人行道出現。

Sidewalks are where people walk between buildings in a city. Besides facilities and trees, there are occasionally parasitic temples. Usually the temple came into existence before the sidewalk.

人造域｜基礎設施界
Domain: **Manmade**
Kingdom: **infrastructure**

人行道族
Tribe: **SIDEWALK**

路旁系列
Along Sidewalk

058
檳榔攤
Betel Nut Stall

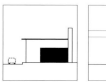

059 → 案例20
電話亭
Call Box

060
烤地瓜爐
Sweet Potato Oven

牆旁系列
Along Wall

061
牆內
Inhabit Wall

062
典型
Typical

063
有拱廊
Arcarde

064
簡易雨遮
Minimal

065 → 案例21
陸橋下
Under Pedestrian Bridge

人群聚集成了聚落，聚落發展引入了車輛。無論是原有的道路拓寬或是新設的都市道路切分，每一筆都是都市發展的痕跡。廟的寄生型態也因此在這族出現多樣的種類：路旁系列與路中系列，路中系列還能分出上中下的分支。

People gather to form settlements and bring cars. Whether broadening the existing roads or building new ones, they are all traces of urban development. Therefore, there are many types in this category of parasitic temples, including the one at the roadside and the one in the middle of the road. The later even grows three families: above the road, on the road, and under the road.

人造域｜基礎設施界
Domain: **Manmade**
Kingdom: **infrastructure**

道路族
Tribe: **ROAD**

路旁系列
Along Edge

066 → 案例22
寵物屋
Pet House

067
警衛亭
Guard House

068
鳥籠
Bird Cage

069
路兩側
Road Both Sides

070
路兩側有頂
Road Both Sides
with Canopy

071
路口兩側
Temple and Oven
Isolated by Road

路中系列
Middle of Road

路面中
In Middle

072 → 案例23
圓環
Roundabout

073
岔路
Crossy

074
路中
In Middle

075
分隔島
On Split

路之上
Above Road

076 → 案例24
路上
Above Road

路之下
Under Road

077 → 案例25
路下
Under
Road

台灣河流短、流速急，而且隨著颱風、暴雨水位上升，周遭很容易積水氾濫。於是在人口聚集的聚落及河流間建造了河堤，原先在河旁的寄生廟也因河堤阻隔而出現在河堤兩側。

Rivers in Taiwan are short and flow fast. When a typhoon or rainstorm hits, water comes in and the nearby areas are often flooded; hence levees are built between the river and settlements. Parasitic temples on the riverbank, therefore, are separated by the levee, and sometimes even survive on both sides.

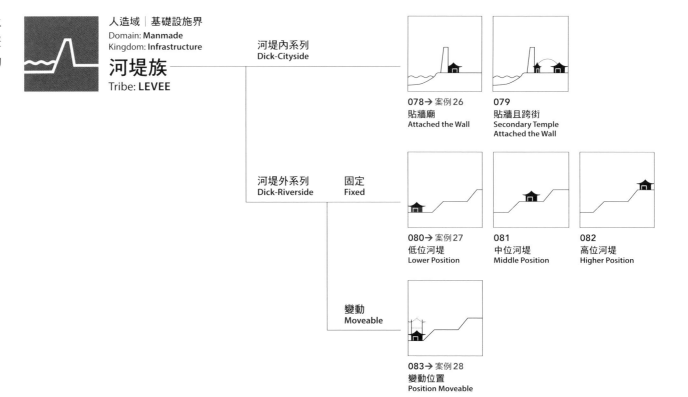

人造域｜基礎設施界
Domain: **Manmade**
Kingdom: **Infrastructure**

河堤族
Tribe: **LEVEE**

河堤內系列
Dick-Cityside

河堤外系列
Dick-Riverside

固定
Fixed

變動
Moveable

078 → 案例 26
貼牆廟
Attached the Wall

079
貼牆且跨街
Secondary Temple
Attached the Wall

080 → 案例 27
低位河堤
Lower Position

081
中位河堤
Middle Position

082
高位河堤
Higher Position

083 → 案例 28
變動位置
Position Moveable

都市與山林常常以擋土牆作為其間的邊界，防止土石崩塌。在這樣的邊緣隙地空間，也是廟宇寄生的所在。

The urban and mountain areas often use retaining walls as their borders to prevent landslide. Sometimes temples find their hosts along the borderline.

人造域｜基礎設施界
Domain: **Manmade**
Kingdom: **Infrastructure**

擋土牆族
Tribe: **RETAINING WALL**

084
低位
Lower Position

085 → 案例 29
中位
Middle Position

086
高位
Higher Position

087
擋土牆下
Under the
Retaining Wall

橋梁架高於地面上，提供車輛快速連接兩個或多個地點；但也切開了地面兩側原有的聯繫。橋下空間零碎，但有廟宇寄生在其中。

Overpasses are elevated to provide a quick link of traffic, but they also cut the ground under it. Space under the bridge is fragmented, while some parasitic temples reside there.

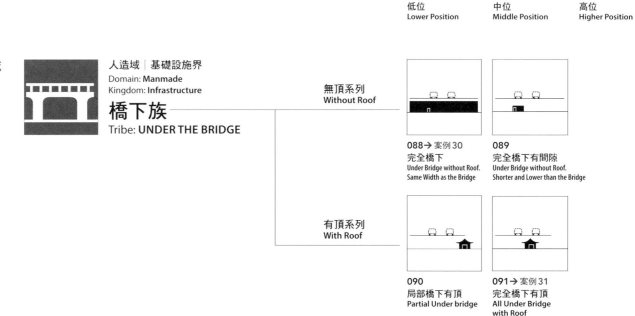

人造域｜基礎設施界
Domain: **Manmade**
Kingdom: **Infrastructure**

橋下族
Tribe: **UNDER THE BRIDGE**

無頂系列
Without Roof

有頂系列
With Roof

088 → 案例 30
完全橋下
Under Bridge without Roof.
Same Width as the Bridge

089
完全橋下有間隙
Under Bridge without Roof.
Shorter and Lower than the Bridge

090
局部橋下有頂
Partial Under bridge

091 → 案例 31
完全橋下有頂
All Under Bridge
with Roof

都市空間非建築物的開放空間中，屬非正式、沒有明確範圍的剩餘空間，可區分成兩者：被道路和建築圍夾出的畸零空間，以及建築間的夾縫。這些非正式空間中都有寄生廟的存在。

The open space outside buildings in a city is informal and unidentified, which can be grouped into two categories: space among roads and buildings, and space between buildings. Parasitic temples also exist in this informal space.

人造域｜都市空間界
Domain: **Manmade**
Kingdom: **Urban Open Space**

剩餘空間族
Tribe: **FRAGMENT**

畸零系列
Marginal Land

   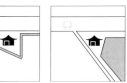

092
雙路畸零地
Cut by two Streets

093
雙路畸零地(公園)
Cut by two Streets and Park

094
單路與牆畸零地
Cut by Street and Wall

095
單路與人行道畸零地
Cut by Road and Pedestrian Path

096 → 案例32
雙路擠出畸零地
Extruded

097
單邊車棚有頂
Garage Extension

夾縫系列
Gap

098 → 案例33
建築間小夾縫
Small Gap Between Buildings

099
建築間小夾縫有頂
Small Gap Between Buildings with canopy

100
建築間中夾縫
Medium Gap Between Buildings

101
建築間大夾縫
Big Gap Between Buildings

公園是都市中正式的開放空間及休憩場所。此類寄生廟通常比公園更早存在；廟宇或部分廟埕是後來才被畫定成公園的一部分的。

Parks are formal open space and recreational places. Parasitic temples here usually came before the parks. The temples or part of its squares are later reassigned to the parks.

人造域｜都市空間界
Domain: **Manmade**
Kingdom: **Urban Open Space**

公園族
Tribe: **PARK**

102
面向公園
Face to Park

103
背向公園
Back to Park

104 → 案例34
公園中
In the Park

寄生廟的族群除了寄生在固定的城市及自然物件之外，現代更演化出可移動性，甚至寄生在各種交通工具上的寄生廟。

Parasitic temples find their hosts in natural objects or fixed places in a city. In modern times, they even develop mobility by parasitizing upon different means of transportation.

人造域｜移動物件界
Domain: **Manmade**
Kingdom: **Mobile Object**

機動族
Tribe: **PORTABLE**

海上系列
Waterside

105 → 案例35
船
Boat

陸上系列
Landside

 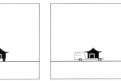

106
三輪車
Tricycle

107 → 案例36
攤車
Street Vender

108
卡車
Truck

6

廟等角透視圖
36＋1案例
Isometric Diagrams

36廟台灣位置圖

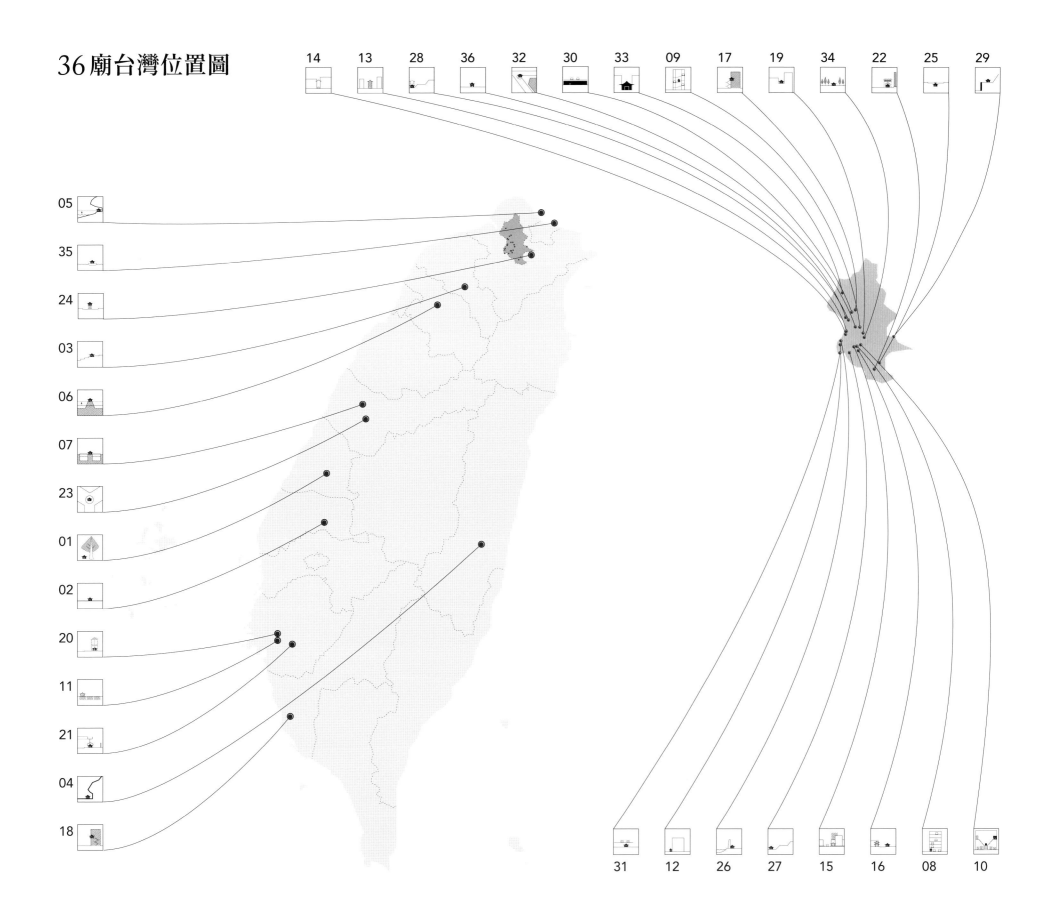

1

樹冠下廟
Tree Temple

彰化永靖古樹公

23°55'3.9"N 120°31'3.1"E

彰化永靖鄉古樹公位於縣道142-1永福路上,所寄生的榕樹推估年齡已有210年,樹高15.2公尺,樹冠面積廣達915平方公尺。後當永福路面臨拓寬,居民向老榕樹擲筊後得到共識,保留原址,自此一樹一廟矗立於道路中央。

樹的信仰並非源自佛道信仰,而是出於先民對萬物之靈的崇敬。這類樹廟多於鄉間所見,僅挑選200年的永靖樹廟記錄,以為代表。

Shutougon ("Lord of the Tree") of Yonjing is located on Yonfu Road (Changhua County Highway 142-1). Its host banyan, estimated 210 years old, is 15.2 meters tall with a crown covering 915 square meters. When Yonfu Road was about to be broadened, the residents questioned the old banyan through poe divination and reached a consensus that the temple should be remained in the original place. The tree and the temple have been standing in the middle of the road thereafter.

Worshipping trees does not originated from Buddhism but ancestors' reverence for the spirit of all things. This kind of tree temple is mostly seen in the countryside. Here we choose the two-hundred-year-old Yonjing Tree Temple as an example of a natural host to a parasitic temple.

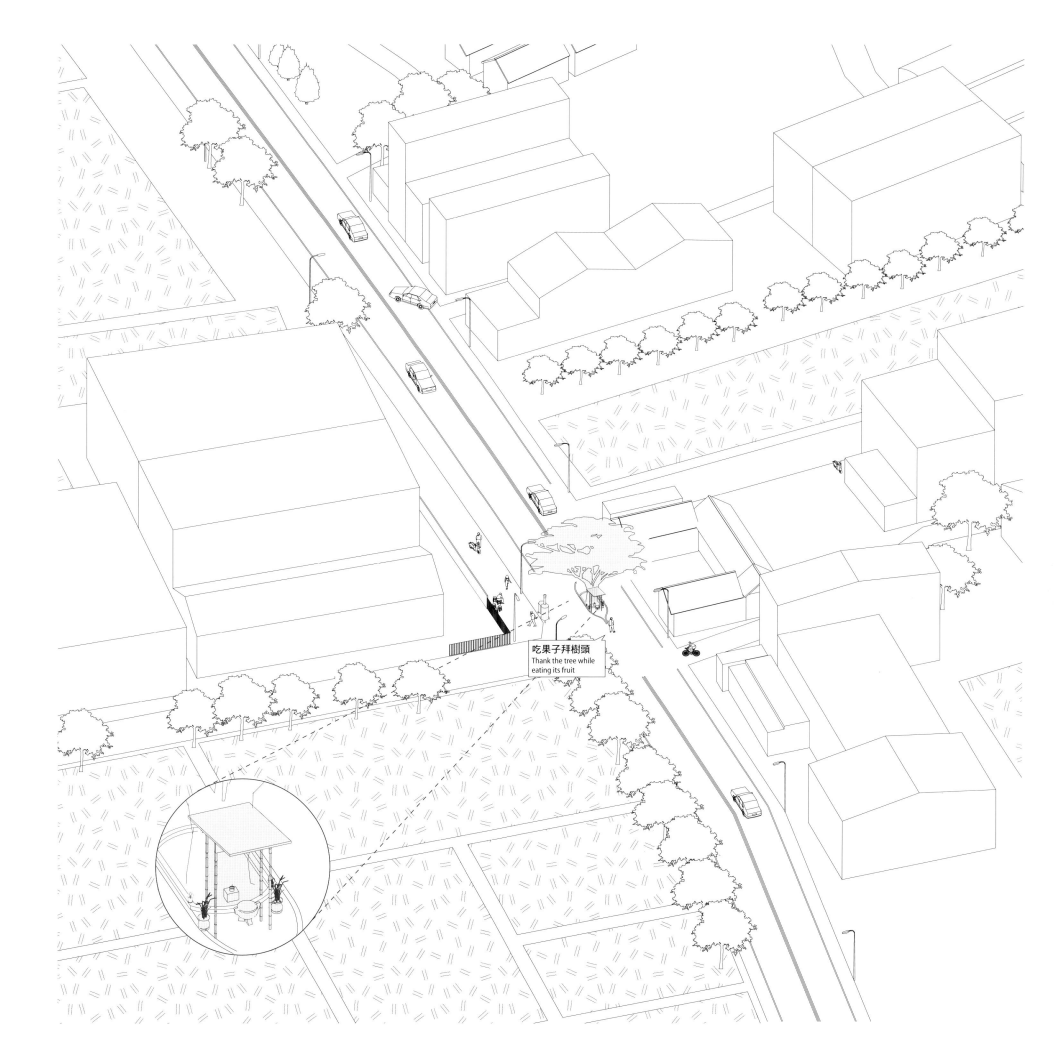

吃果子拜樹頭
Thank the tree while eating its fruit

2
田中廟
Field Temple

苗栗苑裡福德祠

苗 47-1

24°24'56.8"N 120°39'08.8"E

SM

此廟只是從台灣千千萬萬田野中的土地公廟選出的一個代表。有句俗話說：「田頭田尾土地公」，由此可見土地公廟在台灣田野普遍存在的情形，田野中的土地公廟一直都是台灣農業地景的一部分，許許多多的民間故事與傳說也是圍繞著田野中的土地公廟發生。建造土地公廟時的座向反映出「肥水不落外人田」的心理。土地公廟除了看護家園外，也庇護一方居民和物產豐收，所以，當你在田野中看到小小的土地公廟時，千萬別小看祂，祂代表的可是生生不息的希望。

This one is only an example of hundreds of thousands of Tudigong ("Lord of the Soil and the Ground") temples. As the old saying goes, "There are Tudigongs both at the front and the back of a paddy field." It quite summarizes the phenomenon that Tudigong temples commonly exist around the fields in Taiwan, which has been a typical part of local agricultural landscapes and a frequent scene of numerous folk tales and legends. The orientation of the temple reflects the philosophy of "keeping the goodies within the family" when it was under construction. Tudigong not only protects people and guards their home but also blesses them with a bumper harvest. So, when you see a tiny Tudigong temple in the fields, never underestimate Him, for what He represents is endless hope.

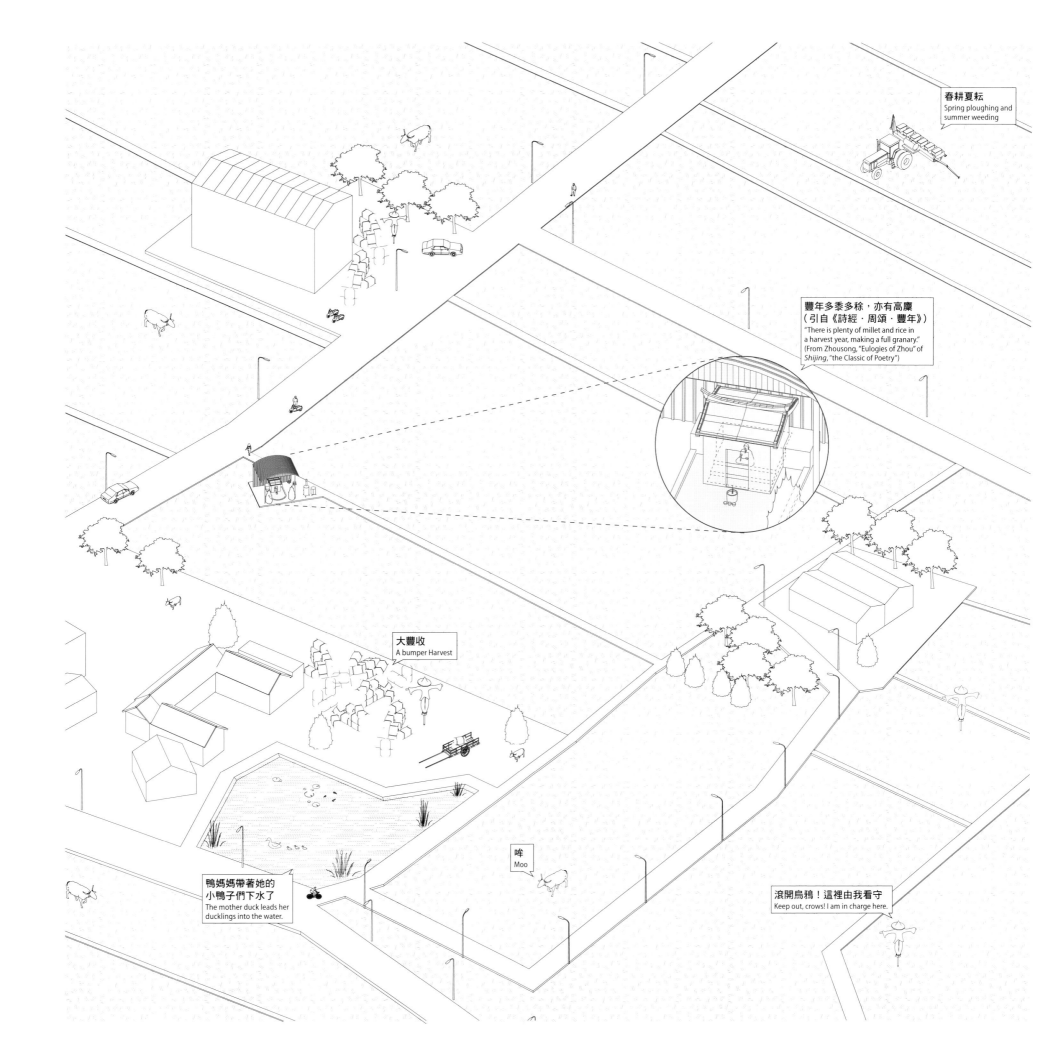

3

梯田廟
Step Field Temple

新竹芎林土地公廟

24°44'50.4"N 121°8'56.2"E

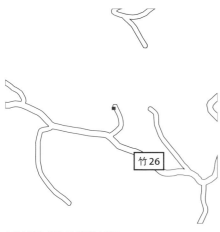

SM

台灣是個島，有70%的土地皆為山林；漢人在遷移的過程中從平原區域逐漸擴張到丘陵地區域。清朝時期，客家人逐漸移墾到新竹縣芎林，每到一處新開墾地時，尊重神靈的客家人常會立伯公祭拜以祈求作物豐收。

梯田是整理過的階梯草坪，下面有藏一個水池。此廟寄生在台灣山林的農業地景梯田及民居間，照看著家園。

Taiwan is an island with about 70 percent of the total land area being covered by forest. The Han people expanded from the plains to the hills during migration. In the Qing Dynasty, the Hakkas started to cultivate in Qionglin, Hsinchu. The local Hakkas particularly respected deities. Whenever they reclaimed an area, they would deify a lord to worship, praying for blessings and harvests.

This terrace is a series of successively receding platforms on a slope cut with a pond below. This temple parasitizes among terraced paddy fields and residential areas in the mountainous region in Taiwan, watching over its territory through the woods.

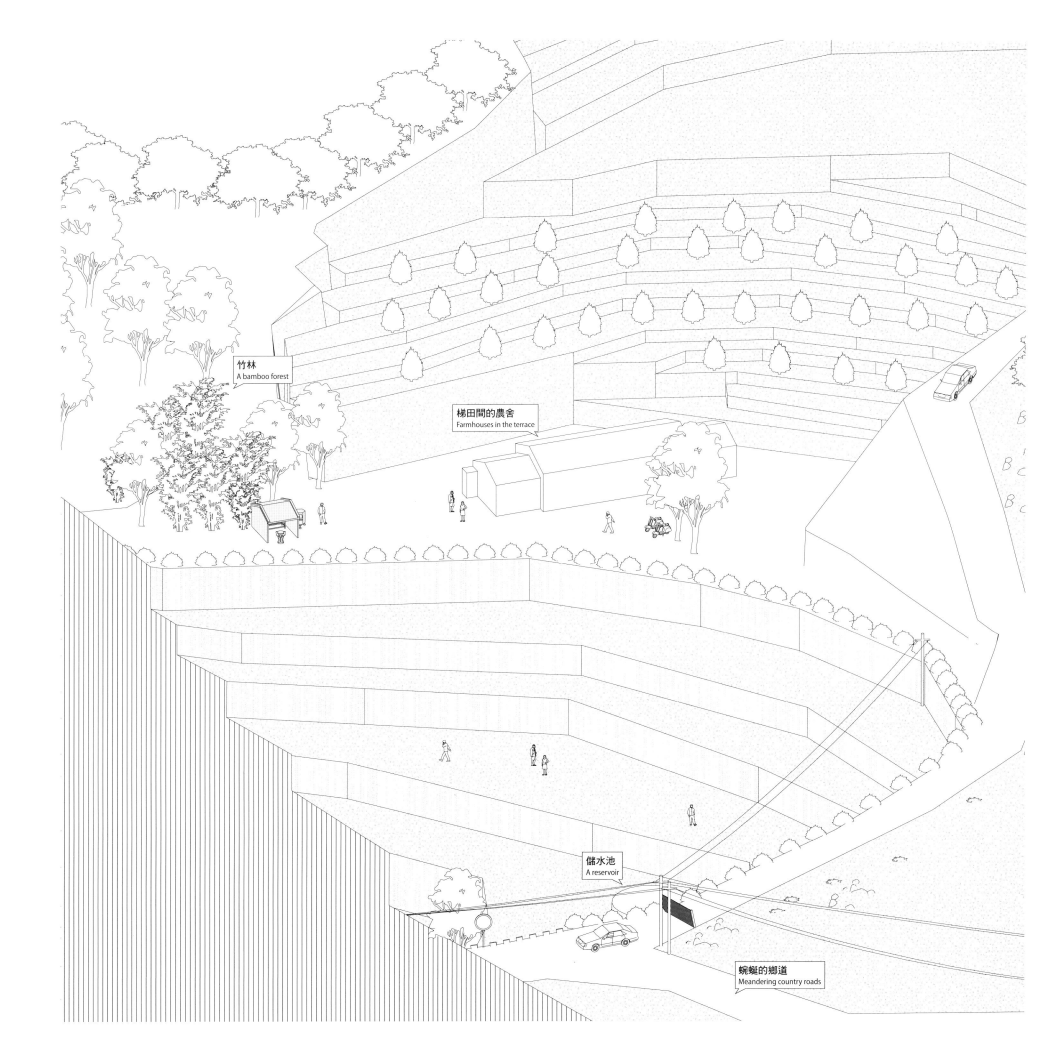

竹林
A bamboo forest

梯田間的農舍
Farmhouses in the terrace

儲水池
A reservoir

蜿蜒的鄉道
Meandering country roads

4

半石中廟
Cave Temple

花蓮虎頭山青龍王洞廟

此廟為花蓮虎頭山區某石洞中的小祭拜空間，廟的後方有一個供人修行的小石洞。

廟距離虎頭山入口，還需經40分鐘車程至青龍洞外之山林小徑，再步行抵達洞口，仍有許多人慕名而來。

其寄生方式與中國五嶽的廟宇有異曲同工之妙，可謂其精細小巧版本。

This temple, confined to some cave in the Hutou Mountain in Hualien, provides little space for worshiping. There is a small cave in the back of the temple for religious practice.

The temple is quite remote. From the entrance to the Hutou Mountain, there is a 40-minute drive and a walk on a mountain trail to the Qinglong Cave. Nonetheless, it still attracts a lot of people.

The way it parasitizes makes it surprisingly similar to the temples in the Five Great Mountains in China, making it like their miniature.

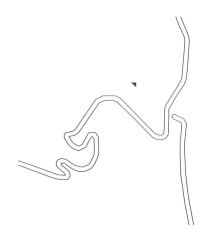

23°31'28.3"N 121°20'25.6"E

XS

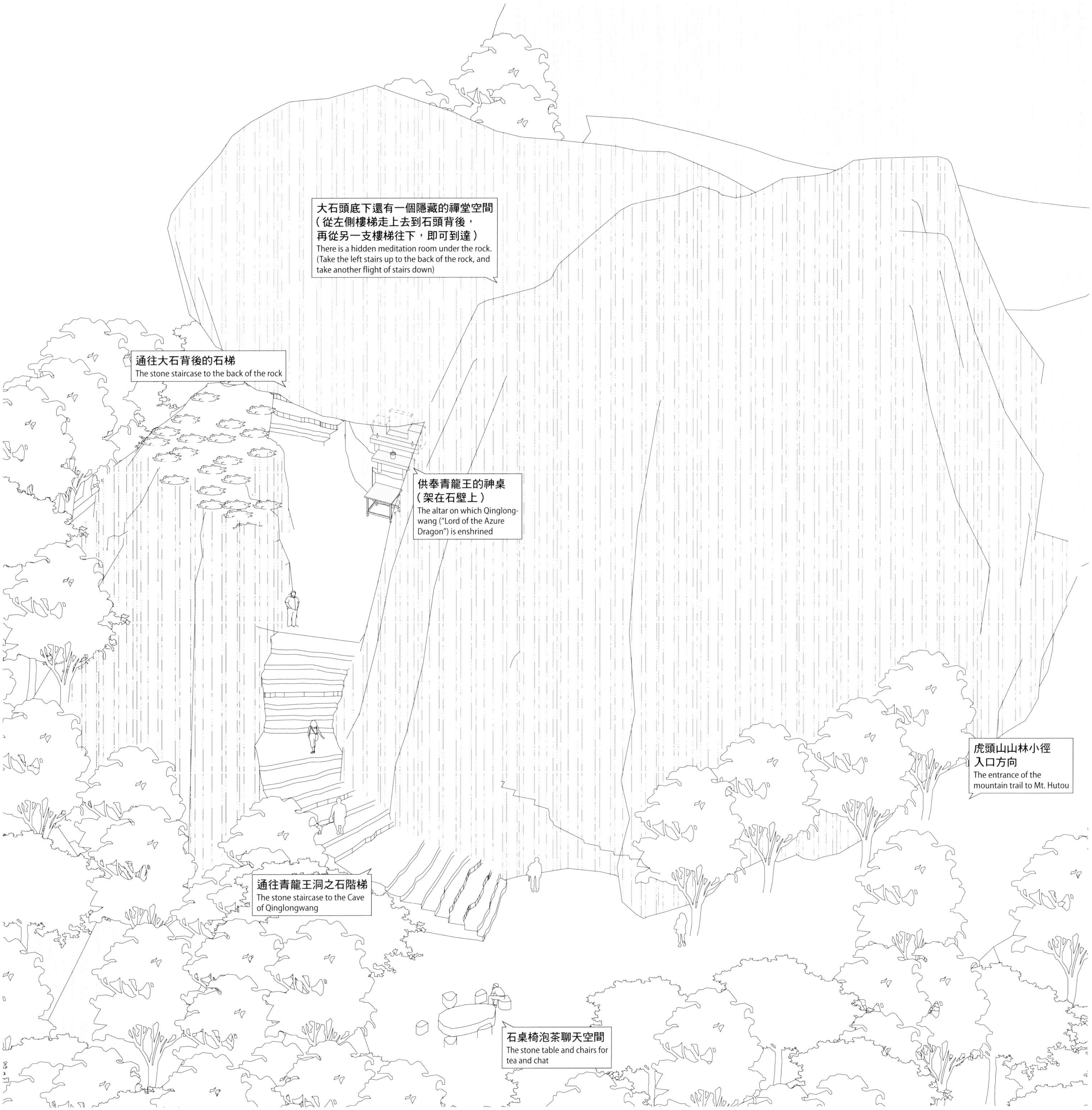

大石頭底下還有一個隱藏的禪堂空間
（從左側樓梯走上去到石頭背後，
再從另一支樓梯往下，即可到達）
There is a hidden meditation room under the rock.
(Take the left stairs up to the back of the rock, and
take another flight of stairs down)

通往大石背後的石梯
The stone staircase to the back of the rock

供奉青龍王的神桌
（架在石壁上）
The altar on which Qinglongwang ("Lord of the Azure
Dragon") is enshrined

虎頭山山林小徑
入口方向
The entrance of the
mountain trail to Mt. Hutou

通往青龍王洞之石階梯
The stone staircase to the Cave
of Qinglongwang

石桌椅泡茶聊天空間
The stone table and chairs for
tea and chat

5

海蝕洞中廟
Erosion Temple

新北金山慈護宮

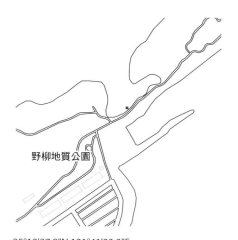

野柳地質公園

25°12'27.8"N 121°41'33.3"E

相傳在清朝嘉慶年間，一尊媽祖神像突然漂到現今野柳地質公園內的媽祖洞，原本只是在洞中設壇祭拜的野柳人興起建廟想法，後來因媽祖託夢改由金山人在金包里街立廟。

幾經協商，野柳人和金山人達成共識，每年請媽祖回到當年發現神像的海蝕洞中做客，以供野柳人祭拜。兩百多年來，金包里二媽每年在農曆四月十六日大退潮時，回到野柳地質公園媽祖洞作客的慶典活動，一直延續到今日。這說明了寄生的狀態是變動的，即使只有一天，無論是從宿主本身，或是從時間軸來看，從來都不是穩定不變。

Mazu Temple in Jinshan can be traced back to the beginning of Jiaqing's reign in the Qing Dynasty. One day, a statue of the sea goddess Mazu floated to a sea cave in Yehliu. People of Yehliu established a temporary shrine in the cave to worship Her. When they were planning to build a temple, Mazu gave specific instructions in dreams that the temple should be located on the Jinbaoli Street. Finally, people of Jinshan built Cihu Temple.

After Mazu left Yehliu, people there missed Her so much that they came to an agreement with Jinshan people that they could invite Mazu back to the sea cave where the statue was found one day every year for Yehliu people to worship Her. For more than two hundred years, Mazu has revisited the cave in the Yehliu Geopark once a year, which becomes a very important local ritual ceremony.

此頁照片均為盧裕源／攝影

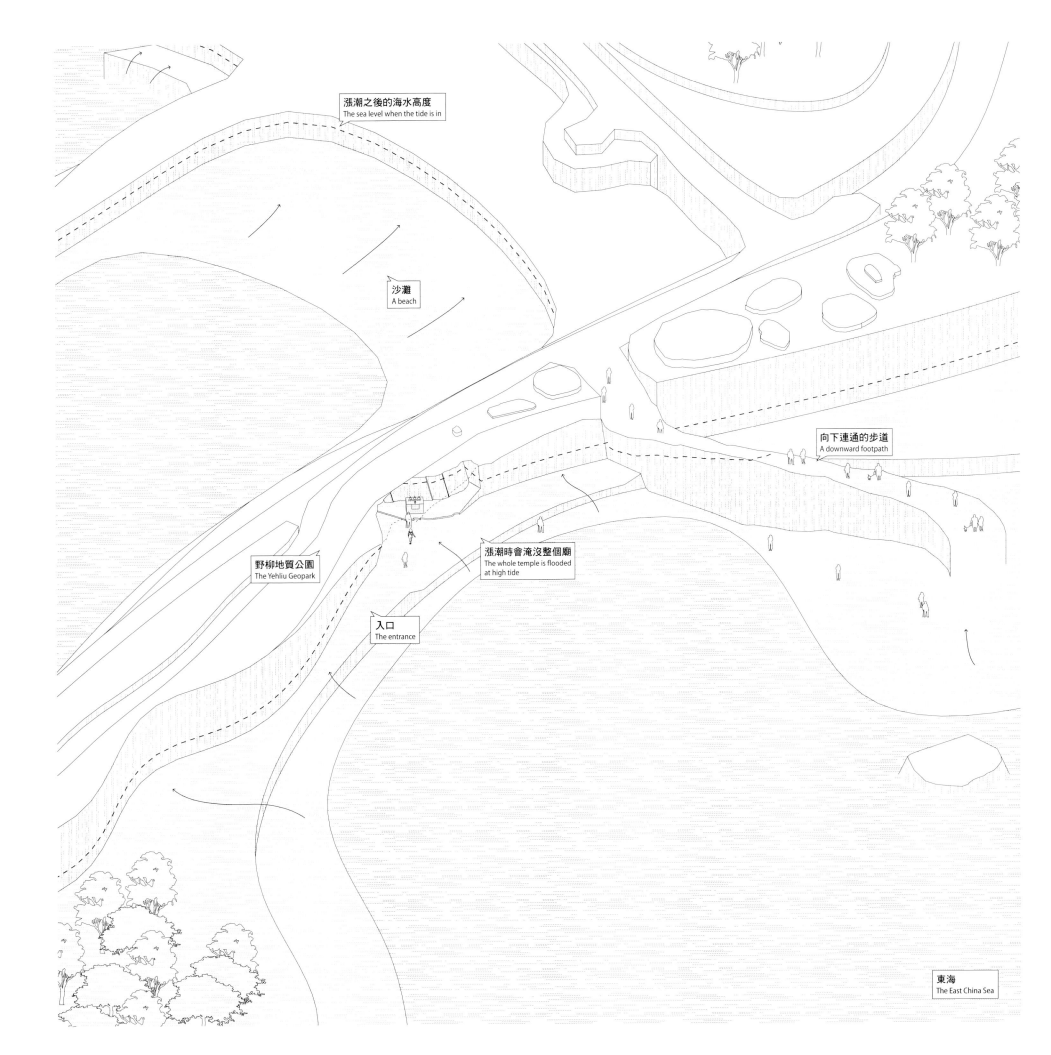

漲潮之後的海水高度
The sea level when the tide is in

沙灘
A beach

向下連通的步道
A downward footpath

野柳地質公園
The Yehliu Geopark

漲潮時會淹沒整個廟
The whole temple is flooded
at high tide

入口
The entrance

東海
The East China Sea

6

池中廟
Island Temple

桃園大溪頭寮水中土地公廟

新福圳

24°50'12.9"N , 121°16'53.8"E

大溪頭寮大池於1967年擴建，擴建範圍內有座土地公廟。原本村民打算進行遷移、另闢新廟，卻在施工期間總遇到機械因不明原因而故障。因此決定採用原地墊高的方式，在大池中建造一座水泥圓形人工島，以保留原土地公廟。而今，訪客只能搭船才能登島參拜。

When Touliao Pond of Dasi was expanded in 1967, a Tudigong temple was within the expansion area. At first, the villagers built a brand-new temple, trying to relocate Tudigong, but got refused. Later, mechanical problems occurred frequently for no apparent reason during construction, so they decided to keep the temple by raising it, building a round concrete artificial island in the pond. Now, visitors can only land on the island by boat.

XXS

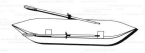

善男信女搭的小船
The boat for devotees

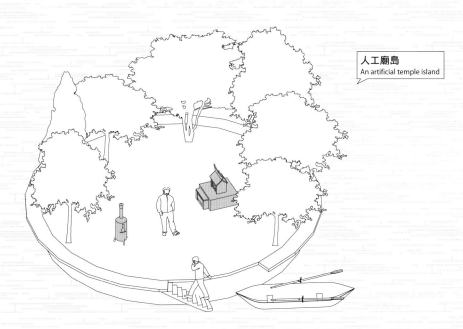

人工廟島
An artificial temple island

低水位季節，人們
可以直接走上島
During low water season, people
can walk directly onto the island.v

新福圳
Xinfu Pond

7

水上廟
Water Temple

台中豐原角潭福德祠

豐原這座全台唯一一座建在水道分隔島上的土地公廟——角潭福德祠，是水道寄生廟中最具代表性的案例。台灣中部主要的灌溉來源之一葫蘆墩圳引水流到西汴幹線，水渠在廟島附近分成兩條，一條往東流向市區，另一條往西流向圳寮里。分隔島上為什麼會有土地公廟？相傳是在日治時期進行整修工程時，一位工程師將一尊隨水漂流而來的神像拾起供奉，工程得以順利完工，之後便蓋廟安置神像，成為圳寮庄的守護神。

這座河道分隔島上除了土地公廟外，還有盪鞦韆與高壓電塔，三者湊在這個島上形成一種奇妙的組合。

There is a Tudigong temple near Jiaotan Road and Yuanhuan East Road in Fengyuan District, Taichung. It is said that during Japanese rule, a Taiwanese engineer found a Tudigong idol in the water when he was hired to maintain the Xibian waterway. He placed the idol in the gateway to Zhenliao Village and worshiped Him. Because the construction went very well, the Irrigation Association then built a temple for Tudigong.

The temple divided the water into two halves. The east stream goes downtown and then southwards. The west stream goes into Zhenliao village and then Anli Dashe. There are also a swing and a transmission tower on the water traffic island, making it a bizarre combination.

24°15'39.0"N 120°43'38.2"E

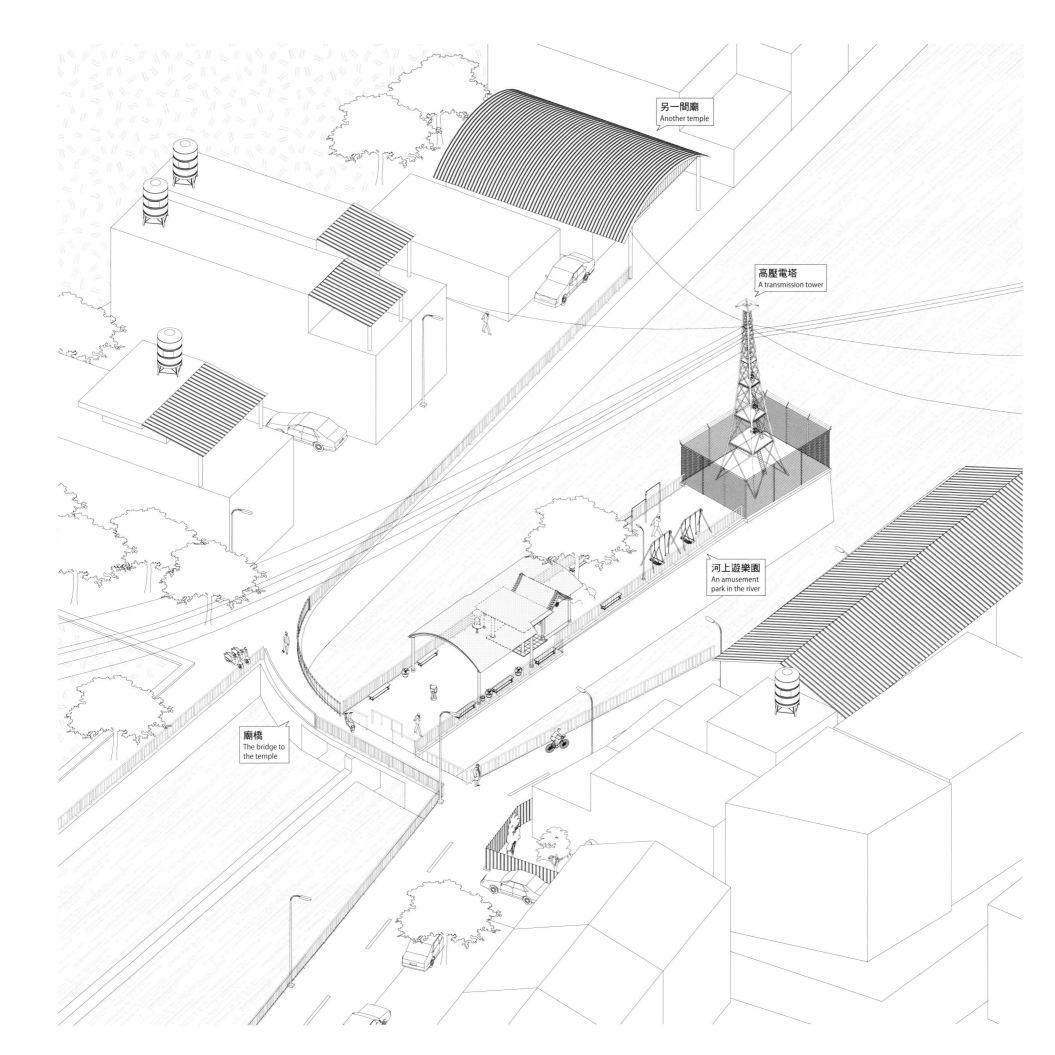

另一間廟
Another temple

高壓電塔
A transmission tower

河上遊樂園
An amusement
park in the river

廟橋
The bridge to
the temple

8

電梯廟
Elevator Temple

台北大安永康四面佛

25°2'0.2"N 121°31'53.4"E

台北永康街四面佛位於熱鬧的永康商圈附近一座停車塔旁一樓，與停車塔共存，大小與停車塔管理員室一致。相較於周遭的都市環境，廟宇不大，僅占據小小的騎樓牆面與騎樓柱，即使一隻柱子的牆面空間也不放過，成為許多許願符與供品的銷售空間。

此廟所祭祀的四面佛文化，與台灣的宗教祭祀存在相當程度的差異，但其在都市中的寄生關係卻與台灣寄生之廟的關係如出一轍，顯見都市寄生的行為，與台灣都市的關係大於宗教本身。

The Four-Faced Buddha (Phra Phrom) is located in the busy Yongkang commercial district. It is on the first floor, adjacent to a parking garage, and as small as a parking manager's office. Compared to its urban environment, the shrine is not large at all, occupying only a tiny alcove and a nearby column, which is used as a display case of wish cards.

The Phra Phrom culture this temple worships is very different from religion in Taiwan, but the way it parasitizes in the city is exactly the same as what other parasite temples in Taiwan do. We can say that the phenomenon of urban parasite temples has more to do with Taiwan cities than with religion itself.

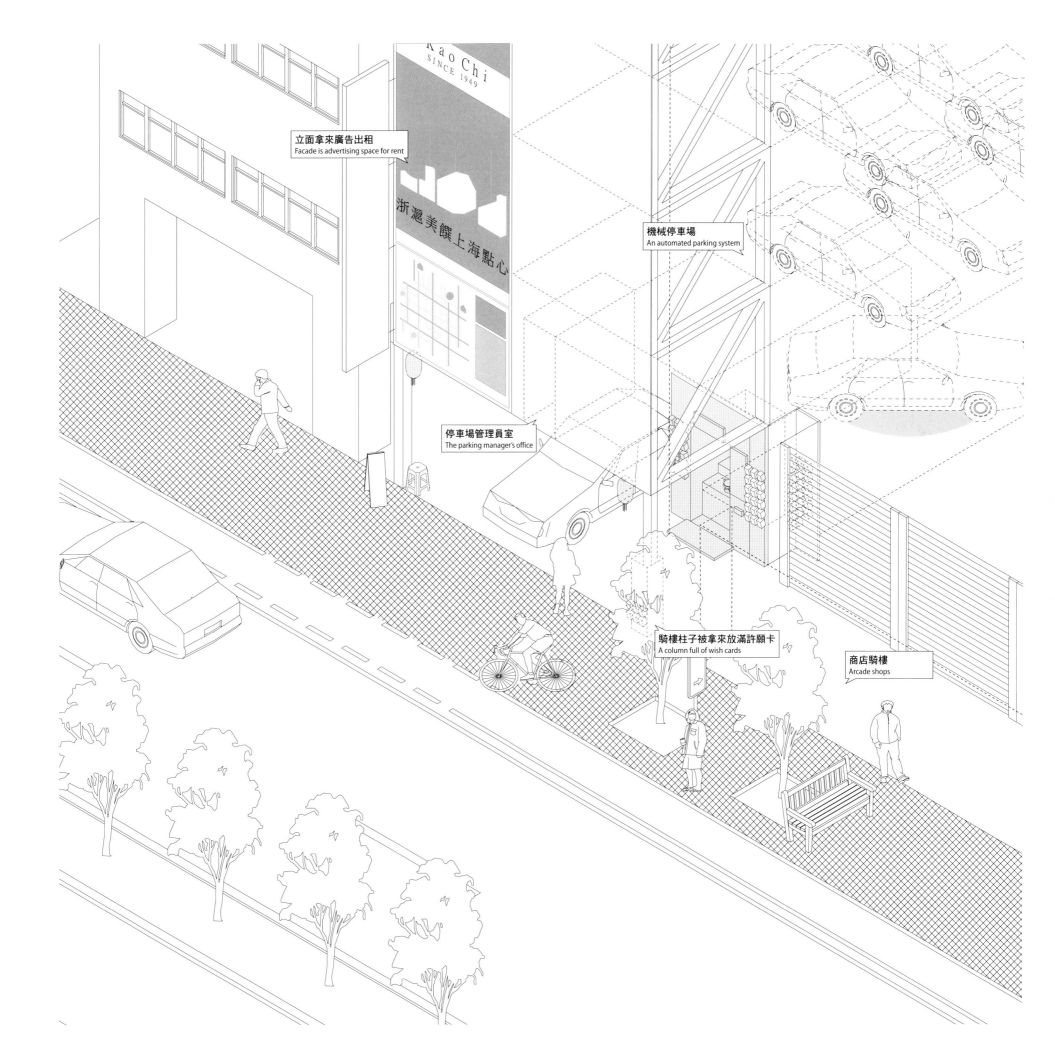

9

停車場迴圈廟
Parking Structure Temple

台北濱江市場福德宮

濱江市場（台北第二果菜批發市場）除了是一個批發市場立體化的先例，也是一個大型的立體停車場，在上下串聯市場的汽車坡道的幾何中心裡有一個福德宮，提供市場裡工作的攤商祭拜，舉辦慶典。

著名的海鮮餐廳「一郎日本料理」就在這個立體批發市場的五樓，所以，開車上餐廳的人都會從上斜坡迴圈的過程中，看見這個福德宮，可說是台灣市場廟中的奇景。

Binjiang Market, aka the Taipei Second Fruit and Vegetable Wholesale Market, was established the soundest and most advanced wholesale system for fresh fruit and vegetable at that time in Taiwan. Its fruit and vegetable supply center provides what supermarkets or caterers need every day. It is also the first multi-story wholesale market, almost like a giant parking garage. In the center of the spiral ramp, there is a Fude Temple for vendors in the market to worship and hold ritual ceremonies.

On the spiral way up to Ichiro Japanese Restaurant, a famous seafood restaurant on the fifth floor of the market, drivers can see this Fude Temple, a wonder of market temples in Taiwan.

25°04'01.6"N , 121°32'12.2"E

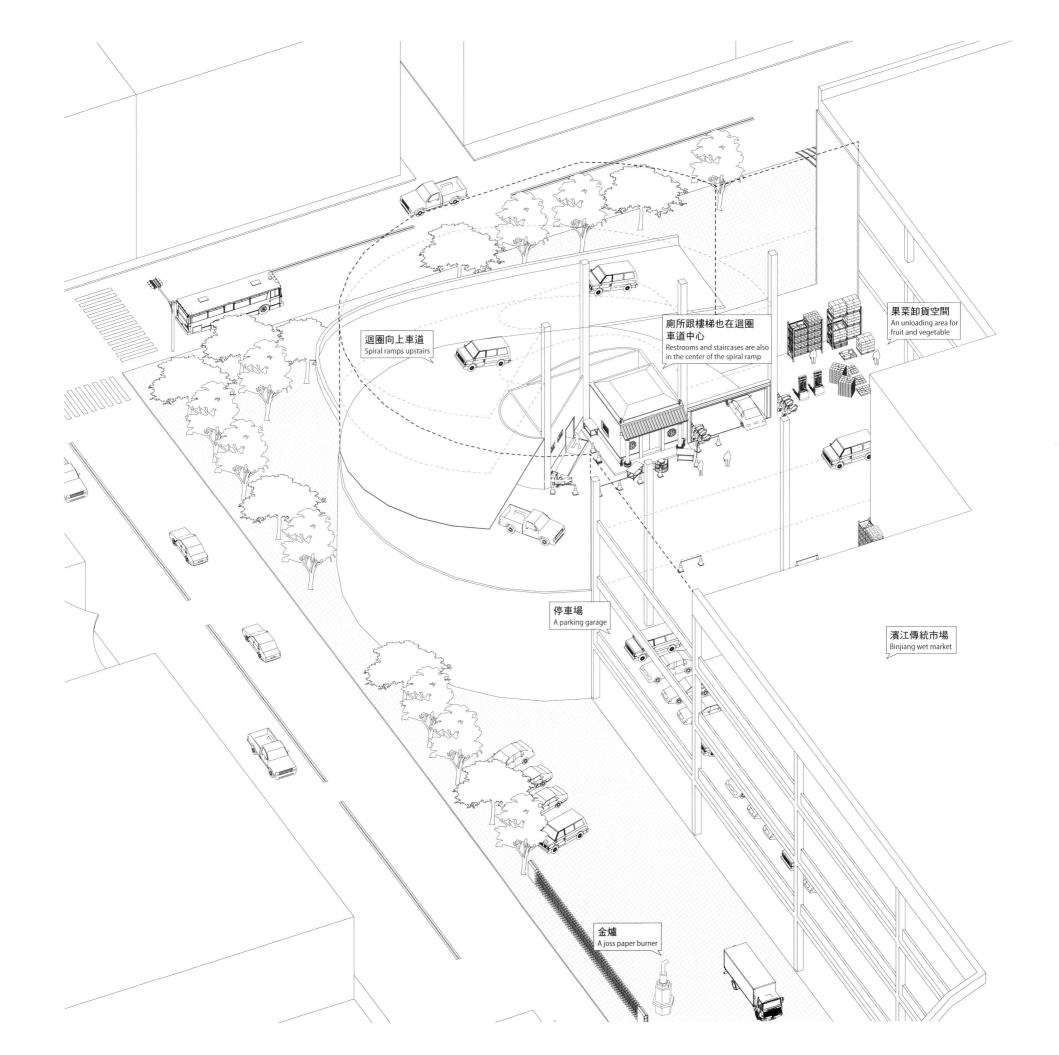

迴圈向上車道
Spiral ramps upstairs

廁所跟樓梯也在迴圈
車道中心
Restrooms and staircases are also
in the center of the spiral ramp

果菜卸貨空間
An unloading area for
fruit and vegetable

停車場
A parking garage

濱江傳統市場
Binjiang wet market

金爐
A joss paper burner

10

市場廟
Market Temple

台北信義市場福德正神

25°02'02.7"N 121°32'20.4"E

位於台北大安區信義路3段107號的信義市場，於60年代興建，鄰近建國花市及大安森林公園，容納了原信義路3段56巷的攤販。

市場內樓中廟在二樓，金爐就放置在通往二樓的階梯平台上，從遠處望去，就像立於市場中心的燈塔。除了從市場中心的兩道折梯以外，透過信義路正門右側的坡道也能直達二樓的廟中。

從早先時期，宮廟周邊因為活動、群眾聚集，逐漸形成市街；近幾十年來，這些市街空地大部分整建更新成市場，如：成功市場、蘭州市場、公館水源市場等。市場由發散型的市街改建為集中式或獨棟的室內市場，原本的信仰空間轉變為一個攤位模矩、供桌直接擺在走廊上的小廟，且多數是祭拜土地公。市場空間速食式的轉變，連帶地將常民的宗教信仰也括進了這個模式之中。

Xinyi Market, built in 1964 to accommodate vendors from Lane 56, Section 3, Xinyi Road, is at 107, Section 3, Xinyi Road, Da'an District, Taipei, near Chien Kuo Weekend Flower Market and Da'an Forest Park.

There is a temple on the second floor, and the joss paper burner is right on the landing below it, which looks like a beacon of the marketplace from a distance. The temple can be accessed by a double staircase in the market or through the ramp on the right side of the main entrance on Xinyi Road.

In early times, people gathered around temples, prompting street markets to gradually develop nearby. However, during recent decades, many scattered street markets have been relocated into certain blocks or even stand-alone buildings, like Chenggong Market, Lanzhou Market, Shuiyuan Market, etc. Consequently, temples got shrunk to the size of a vendor with altars on the hallway, and the deities enshrined are almost Tudigong. It seems that while the markets are under McDonaldization, the local religion cannot exclude itself from the overwhelming trend.

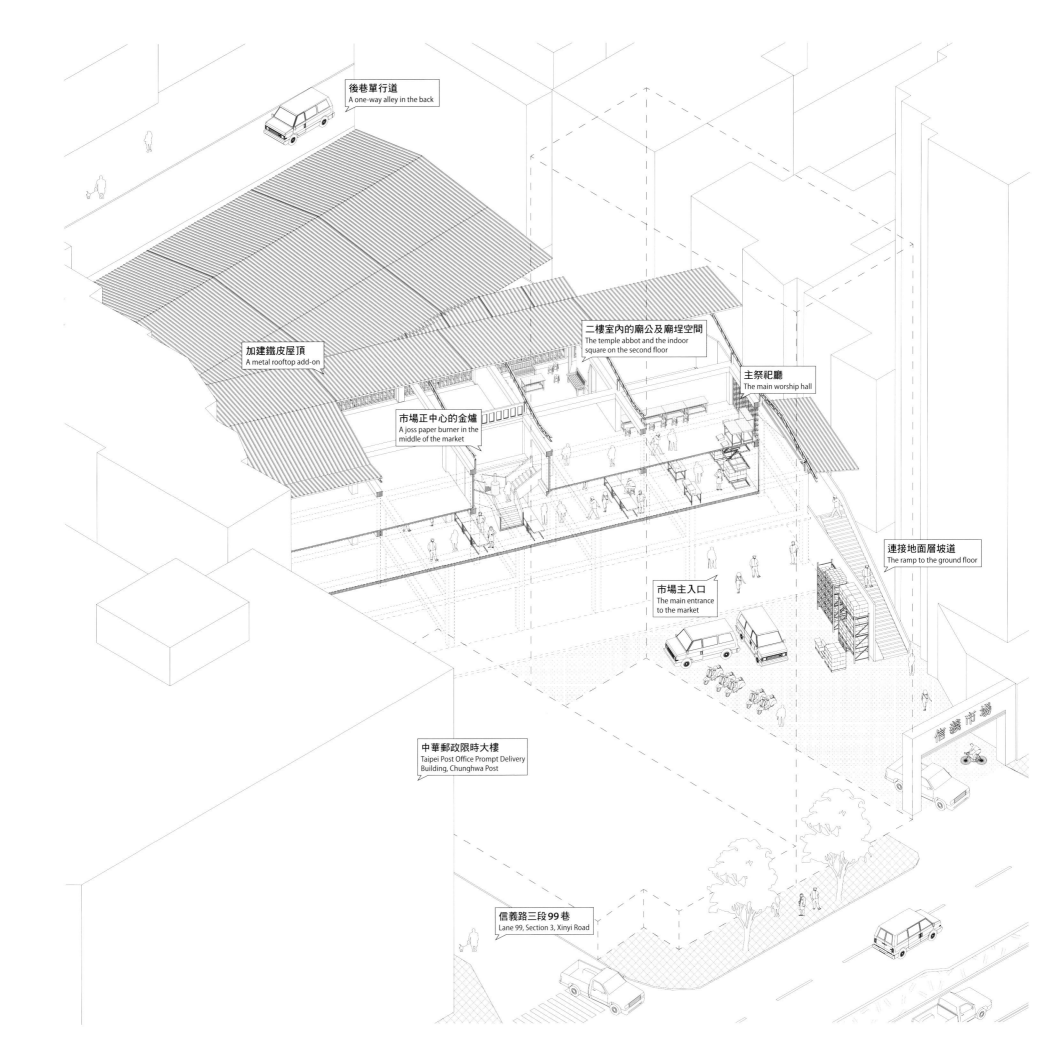

後巷單行道
A one-way alley in the back

加建鐵皮屋頂
A metal rooftop add-on

二樓室內的廟公及廟埕空間
The temple abbot and the indoor square on the second floor

主祭祀廳
The main worship hall

市場正中心的金爐
A joss paper burner in the middle of the market

連接地面層坡道
The ramp to the ground floor

市場主入口
The main entrance to the market

中華郵政限時大樓
Taipei Post Office Prompt Delivery Building, Chunghwa Post

信義路三段 99 巷
Lane 99, Section 3, Xinyi Road

信義市場

11

有露臺廟
Terrace Temple

台南永康開仙宮

開仙宮位於台南永康，建於近10間的平房屋頂之上，擁有廣大的廟埕空間。這10間有它們各自的物業（商業），或許說這廟騎在10間商店上更貼切，在街角最貴最大的店面租給了便利商店。

主廟以兩支對稱的折梯連接一二樓，在跨越四線道的北側三角地也有本廟附屬的小廟、金爐及戲台。

要擁有廣大的廟埕空間，不一定得位於鄉下。

誰說廟埕必然位於一樓？

Kaixian Temple, built on top of ten bungalows in Yonkang, Tainan, has a vast temple square. Each of the ten houses has its own business, and the biggest, most expensive one in the corner is a convenience store. In a way, it is even more proper to say that the temple is on top of ten shops.

The primary temple uses two symmetrical U-shaped staircases to connect to the ground floor. In the triangular traffic island across four lanes north to the primary temple, there sit a tiny secondary temple, a joss paper burner, and an outdoor stage.

It does not have to be in the countryside to own a vast temple square.

And who says that the temple square has to be on the ground?

23°1'23.5"N 120°12'58.1"E

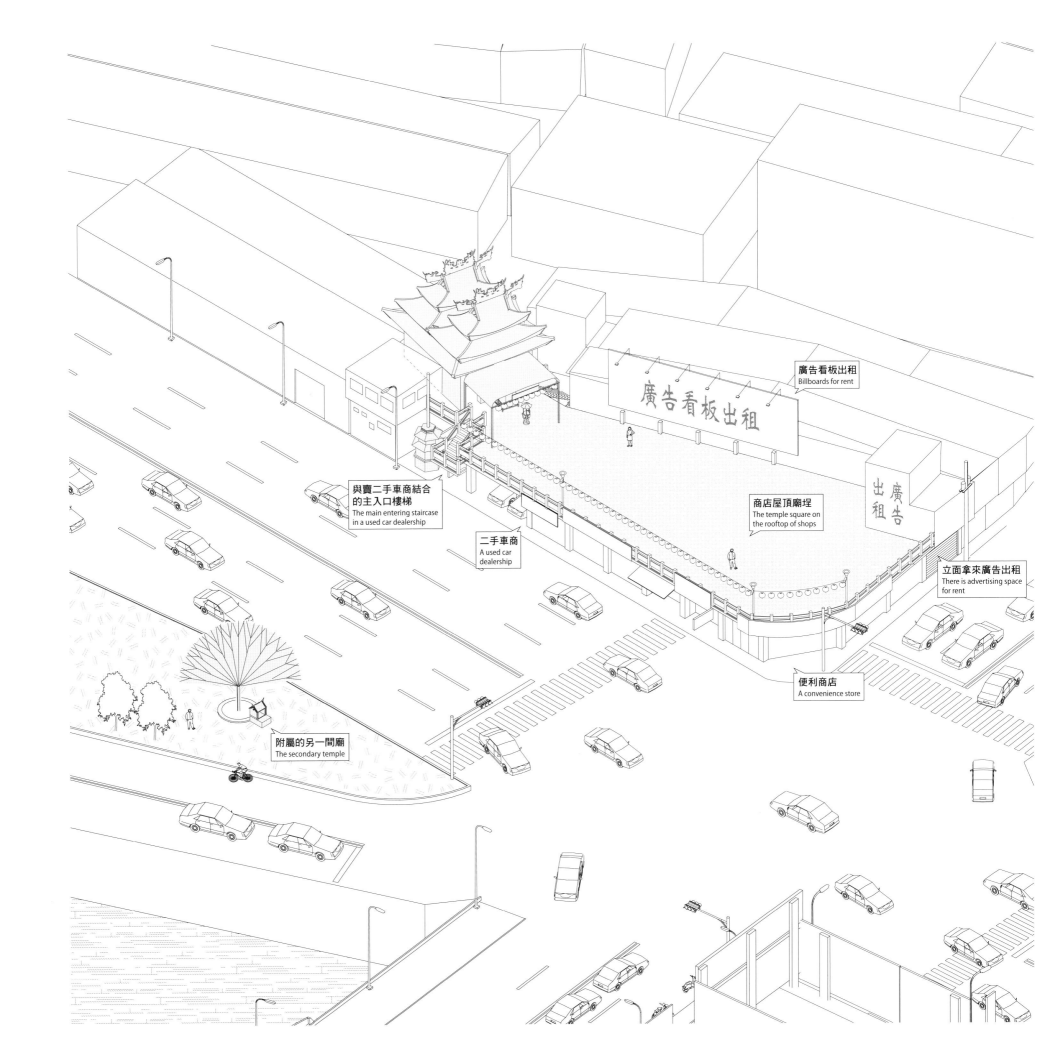

廣告看板出租
Billboards for rent

與賣二手車商結合的主入口樓梯
The main entering staircase in a used car dealership

商店屋頂廟埕
The temple square on the rooftop of shops

出租廣告

立面拿來廣告出租
There is advertising space for rent

二手車商
A used car dealership

便利商店
A convenience store

附屬的另一間廟
The secondary temple

12

透天厝邊廟
Aside House Temple

台北萬華石敢當

25°01'57.2"N 121°29'45.9"E

萬華昔稱「艋舺」，早期因為鄰近淡水河、地理位置佳，與大稻埕形成北台灣重要的市街。本廟處於舊市街通往板橋市中心的主要幹道上。

透天厝邊廟位於艋舺大道336巷道口，幾乎沒有廟體，倚靠著一樓的透天平房外牆而生。即使占地不到5平方公尺，廟的所有基本配備幾乎一應俱全，零散物品也能收納進懸掛在透天厝外牆的壁櫃之中。

近幾年來，本區面臨都市更新的議題。開發商提出50%建蔽率、300%容積率的開發規畫，未來，透天厝邊廟周邊的舊城紋理將不復存在。

在城市追求快速發展的同時，所喪失的或許不只有獨特的文化地景，還有市井小民生活中的心靈寄託。那些暗夜中閃著紅色微光的異質空間，或許象徵著逐漸失去自明性的台灣城市，正發出微弱的求救信號。在圍城之中。

Wanhua, close to Tamsui River, is known historically as Monga. Because its geographic advantage, Wanhua, along with Twatutia, formed important city streets in northern Taiwan in early times. This temple is on the main artery from the old city streets to downtown Banqiao.

Located on the entrance to Lane 336, Bangka Boulevard, this hous-side temple has almost no body, surviving next to an exterior wall of a house. Covering an area of less than five square meters, the temple, surprisingly, has almost all necessary equipment. Small items can even be stored in the cupboard on the wall.

In recent years, this district has been facing the issue of urban renewal. Developers proposed a project with a building coverage ratio of 50% and a floor to area ratio of 300%. In the future, the old buildings around the house-side temple will no longer exist.

While the city is seeking rapid development, not only unique cultural land-scapes may be lost, but also spiritual sustenance of common townspeople. Sieged in urban areas, those heterogeneous places with the red dim glow in the dark maybe symbolize a weak mayday signal of Taiwan cities which are losing their identities.

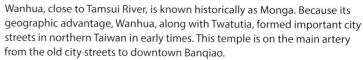

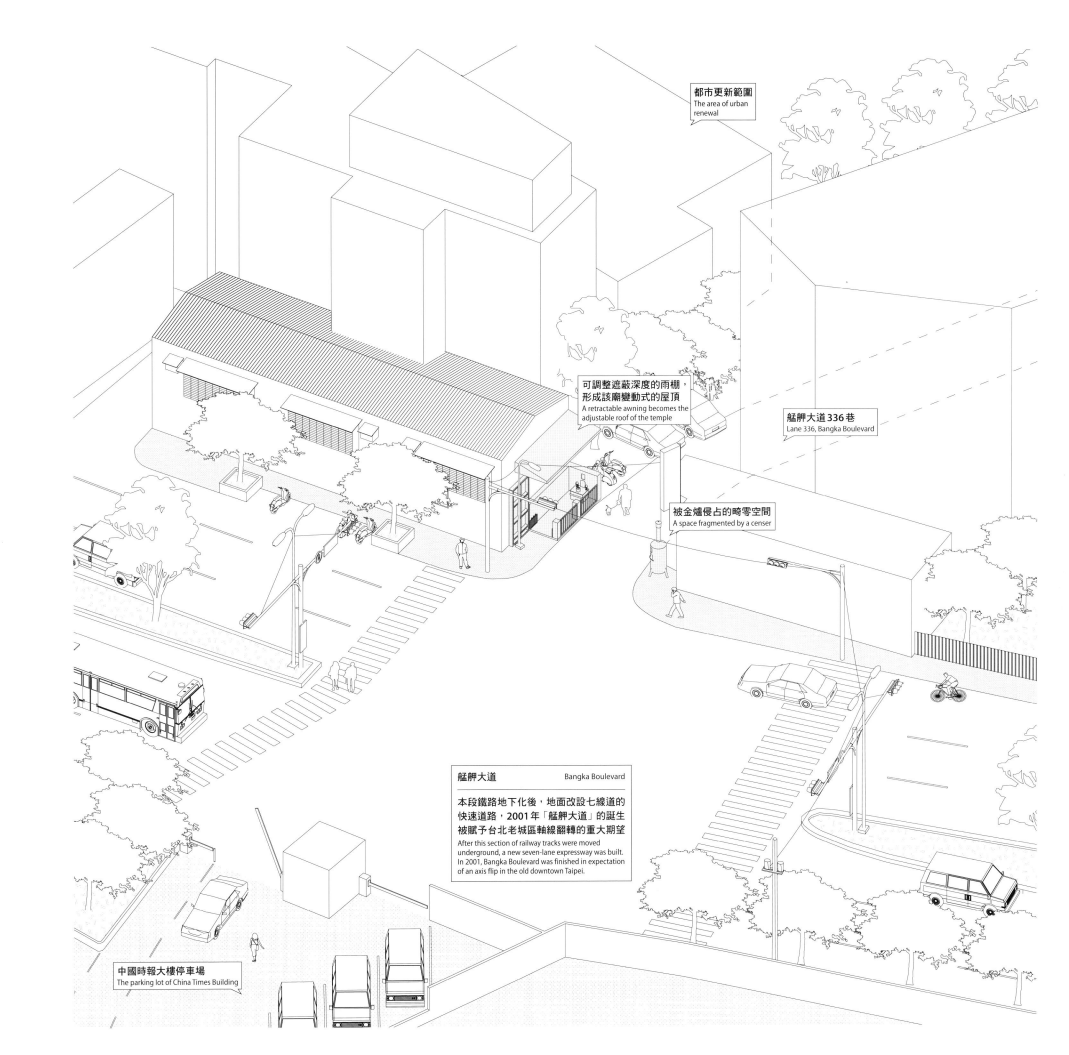

都市更新範圍
The area of urban renewal

可調整遮蔽深度的雨棚，形成該廟變動式的屋頂
A retractable awning becomes the adjustable roof of the temple

艋舺大道 336 巷
Lane 336, Bangka Boulevard

被金爐侵占的畸零空間
A space fragmented by a censer

艋舺大道　　　　Bangka Boulevard

本段鐵路地下化後，地面改設七線道的快速道路，2001 年「艋舺大道」的誕生被賦予台北老城區軸線翻轉的重大期望
After this section of railway tracks were moved underground, a new seven-lane expressway was built. In 2001, Bangka Boulevard was finished in expectation of an axis flip in the old downtown Taipei.

中國時報大樓停車場
The parking lot of China Times Building

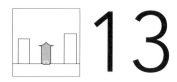

13

跨街廟
Overstreet Temple

台北大同法主公廟

清光緒年間，大稻埕發生瘟疫，法主公顯靈消災而建廟。後來因拓寬道路，便拆掉後殿，只留下前殿。

　台北市大同區法主公廟歷經多代演變與改建，最後一次是1996年由李祖原建築師改建成五層樓建築，一樓大部分空間挑高供巷道穿越，變成一座非常罕見、腳下有車道與車經過的立體廟，二至四樓則為祭祀神明的神殿。此外，整間廟以電梯為主要出入口，緊臨主要道路的北面沒有開窗，對都市來說，可說是沒有表情的建築。

Legend has it that in 1878, a plague broke out in Twatutia. People believed their prayers to Fazhugong subsided the plague, so they donated money to build a temple to show their gratitude. In 1968, the Taipei City Government demolished the back hall when broadening Nanjing West Road, and only the small rectangular front hall survived.

In 1996, the temple was rebuilt into a five-storied building. The first floor has a high ceiling for traffic, and the second to the fourth floors accommodate four shrines. It is noteworthy that there is no window in the north side of the building. The façade design of the temple is rare in Taiwan, plus putting four halls in a tall narrow building and installing an elevator make Fazhugong Temple one of its kind.

25°03'13.8"N 121°30'43.6"E

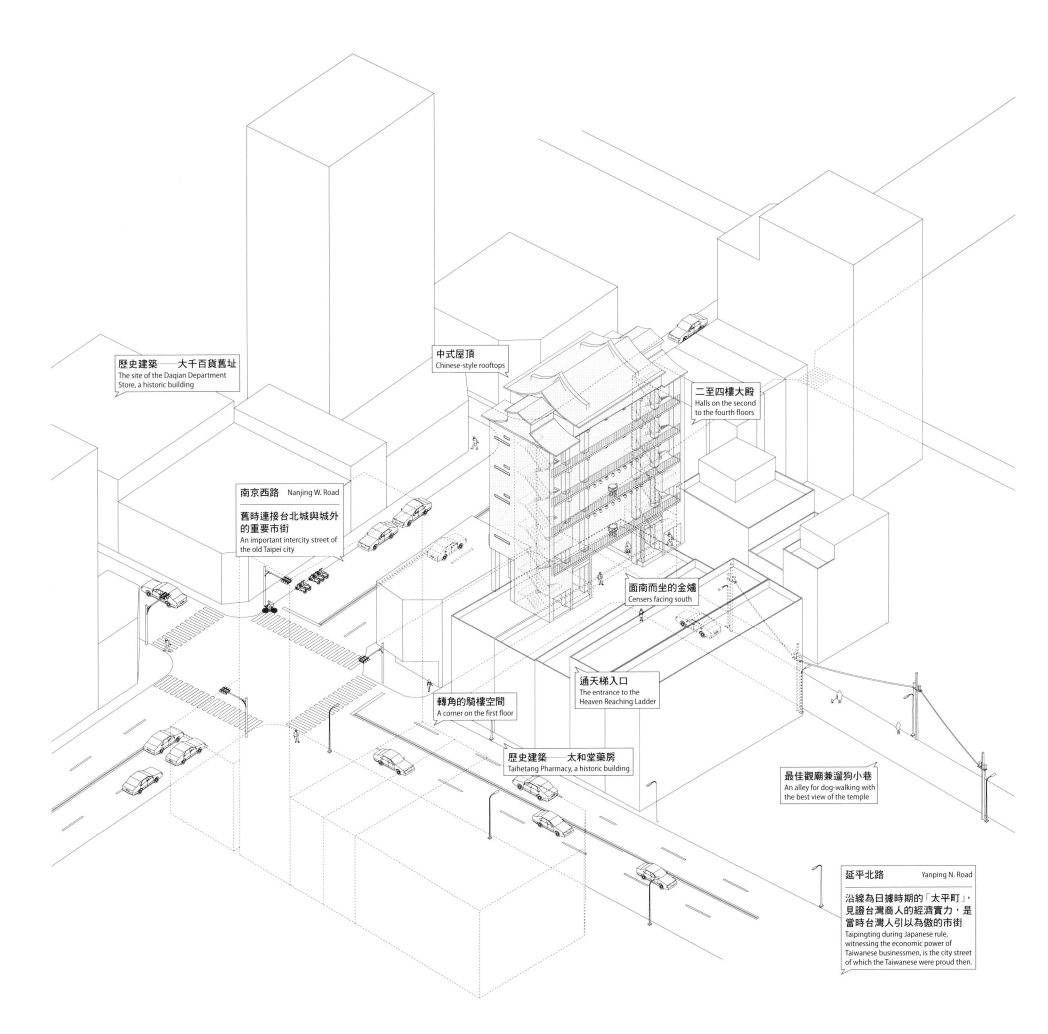

歷史建築──大千百貨舊址
The site of the Daqian Department Store, a historic building

中式屋頂
Chinese-style rooftops

二至四樓大殿
Halls on the second to the fourth floors

南京西路　Nanjing W. Road

舊時連接台北城與城外的重要市街
An important intercity street of the old Taipei city

面南而坐的金爐
Censers facing south

轉角的騎樓空間
A corner on the first floor

通天梯入口
The entrance to the Heaven Reaching Ladder

歷史建築──太和堂藥房
Taihetang Pharmacy, a historic building

最佳觀廟兼遛狗小巷
An alley for dog-walking with the best view of the temple

延平北路　Yanping N. Road

沿線為日據時期的「太平町」，見證台灣商人的經濟實力，是當時台灣人引以為傲的市街
Taipingting during Japanese rule, witnessing the economic power of Taiwanese businessmen, is the city street of which the Taiwanese were proud then.

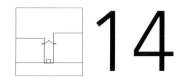

街屋廟
Townhouse Temple

台北大同臺疆樂善壇

25°3'7.6"N 121°30'39.2"E

位於台北市大同區的臺疆樂善壇，是非常典型的仿古廟宇街屋建築，融合了現代建築、傳統語彙與廟宇宮殿式屋頂的混合體。在都市環境中，非常容易找到像它這種因建地有限，而垂直向上發展的立體廟，門樓雖與周邊騎樓結合，卻挑高為兩樓高度，突顯莊嚴氣氛；但也因為沒有廟埕空間，天公爐侵占了騎樓人行道的公共空間。此街屋廟的建築平面空間與標準街屋相類似，和周邊住宅街屋的高度、面積大同小異，但立面卻大量運用宗教建築語彙設計，與左右兩側街屋採一樓店面、其他樓層住家、樓梯位於巷弄側的格局完全不同。

Taijiang Leshantan, is at 263, Chang'an West Road, Datong District, Taipei. Built in 1947, it mocks the architectural style of ancient temples, basing itself on a typical street house in Taipei. The result is a hybrid of modern building, traditional features, and a palace-like rooftop. Nowadays, it is easy to find such kind of uplifting temple since the area of the building site is limited. It also has the arcade, but twice as high as its adjoining counterparts. And its Tian Gong Censer (a censer for the Jade Emperor) under the arcade occupies a part of the public space. Although it kind of merges with the surrounding houses on the street, it is a religious building with a completely different façade which makes it outstanding.

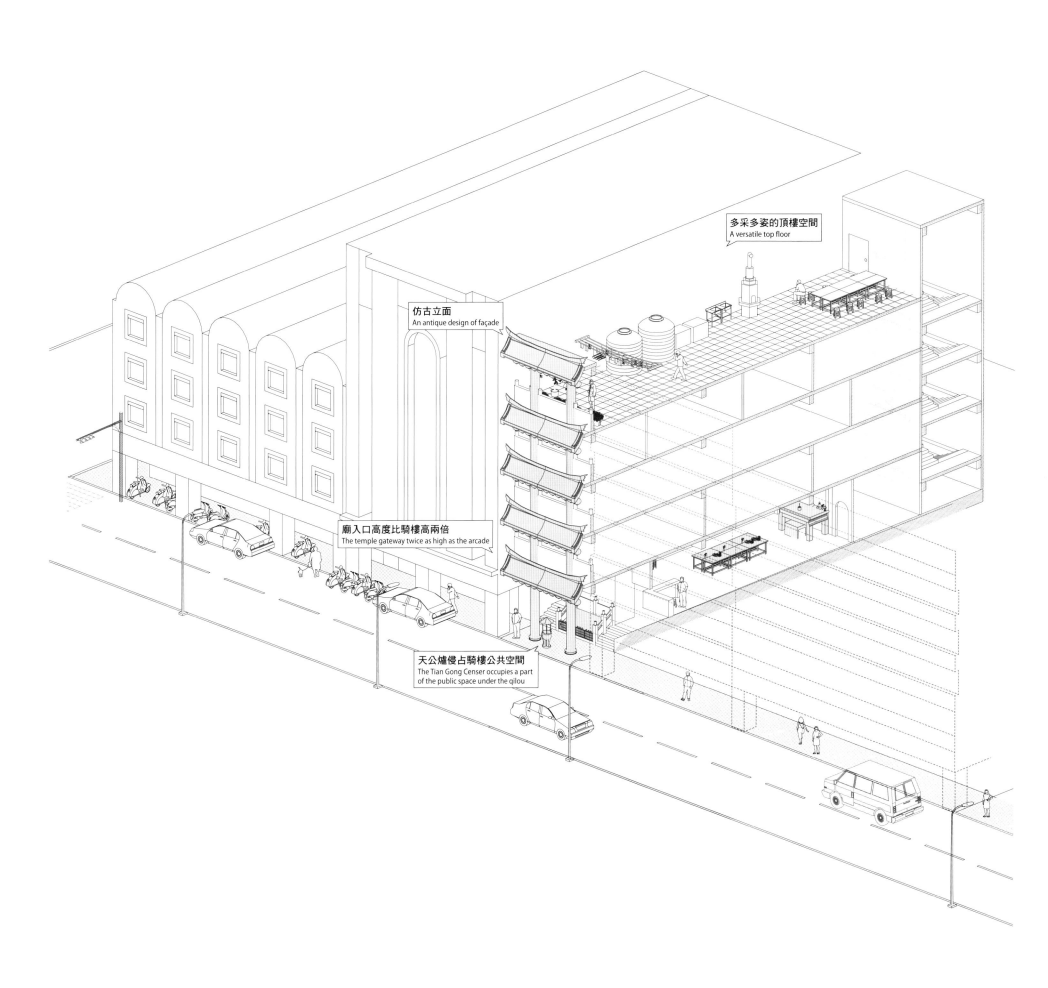

多采多姿的頂樓空間
A versatile top floor

仿古立面
An antique design of façade

廟入口高度比騎樓高兩倍
The temple gateway twice as high as the arcade

天公爐侵占騎樓公共空間
The Tian Gong Censer occupies a part of the public space under the qilou

15

防火巷廟
Alley Temple

台北東門聖母宮

防火巷廟位於台北市東門市場旁的臨沂街66巷中。廟占據一樓，樓深超過10M，向上突出一個假夾層，似乎長出了二樓的祭拜空間。此廟主要祭祀媽祖，外面僅約3M的防火巷又供奉著不同的神祇，多尊神像就隔著人來人往的巷弄互相對望著。

在1979年因為金山街拓寬為金山南路而一分為二的東門市場中，防火巷廟占據一個極不顯眼的空間。面對變遷中的台北城，這間寄生之廟僅藉由一座能遮風避雨的棚子、吊掛著的紅燈籠與面對金山南路的牌樓，暗示其獨特又隱晦的存在。

The alley temple is hidden in Lane 66, Linyi Street, near Dongmen Market. The temple occupies the first floor with a depth of more than 10 meters. There seems to be a second floor for worship, but it is just a decorative mezzanine. The main deity is the sea goddess Mazu, and many other deities are enshrined in the three-meter-long alley outside the temple, looking at one another through the crowd.

In 1979, Jinshan Street was broadened into Jinshan South Road, so Dongmen Market was divided in half. It is in this market that the temple occupies an insignificant spot. Facing the constantly changing Taipei city, the temple marks its special yet secret existence by a sheltering canopy, red lanterns, and a pailou (a Chinese decorated gateway) facing Jinshan South Road.

25°2'5.1"N 121°31'39.3"E

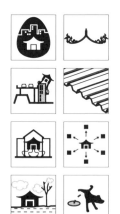

十分隱密的二樓廟，
外人都不得其門而入
A highly secret second floor
not open to the public

與巷弄結合的洗手台與神壇
The sink and the altar combined with the alley

入口與周邊商店騎樓結合
The entrance combined with nearby stores

16

轉角廟
Corner Apartment Temple

台北大安青龍宮

25°01'42.8"N 121°31'59.1"E

青龍宮位於台北市大安區和平東路一段183巷,占地57坪,供奉多位神祇。因為主祀媽祖的保佑,信徒逐年成長。1975年由信徒發起集資,買下現址二樓,並命名青龍宮;1985年,再集資買下今址一樓和地下室,並聘廟祝一人,專責看廟。非常特別的是,該區所屬的青田街區有許多宗教空間,除青龍宮本身,轉角為天主教聖家堂,南側更有全台灣僅六座之一的清真寺。顯見台灣社會有著多元而彼此共融的信仰。

Qinglong Temple, located at Lane 183, Section 1, Heping East Road, Da'an District, Taipei, covers an area of 188.47 square meters and enshrined many deities. Because of blessing of the main deity Mazu, the population of devotees has been growing larger. In 1975, devotees raised money for the purchase of the second floor and named it Qinglong Temple. Ten years later, they did it again to acquire the first floor and the basement, and hired a abbot to manage the temple. It is noteworthy that there are various religious places in the neighborhood. A Holy Family Catholic Church is right in the next block. Taipei Grand Mosque, one of the six mosques in Taiwan, is just a block away. It shows how diversified Taiwan is in terms of religious belief.

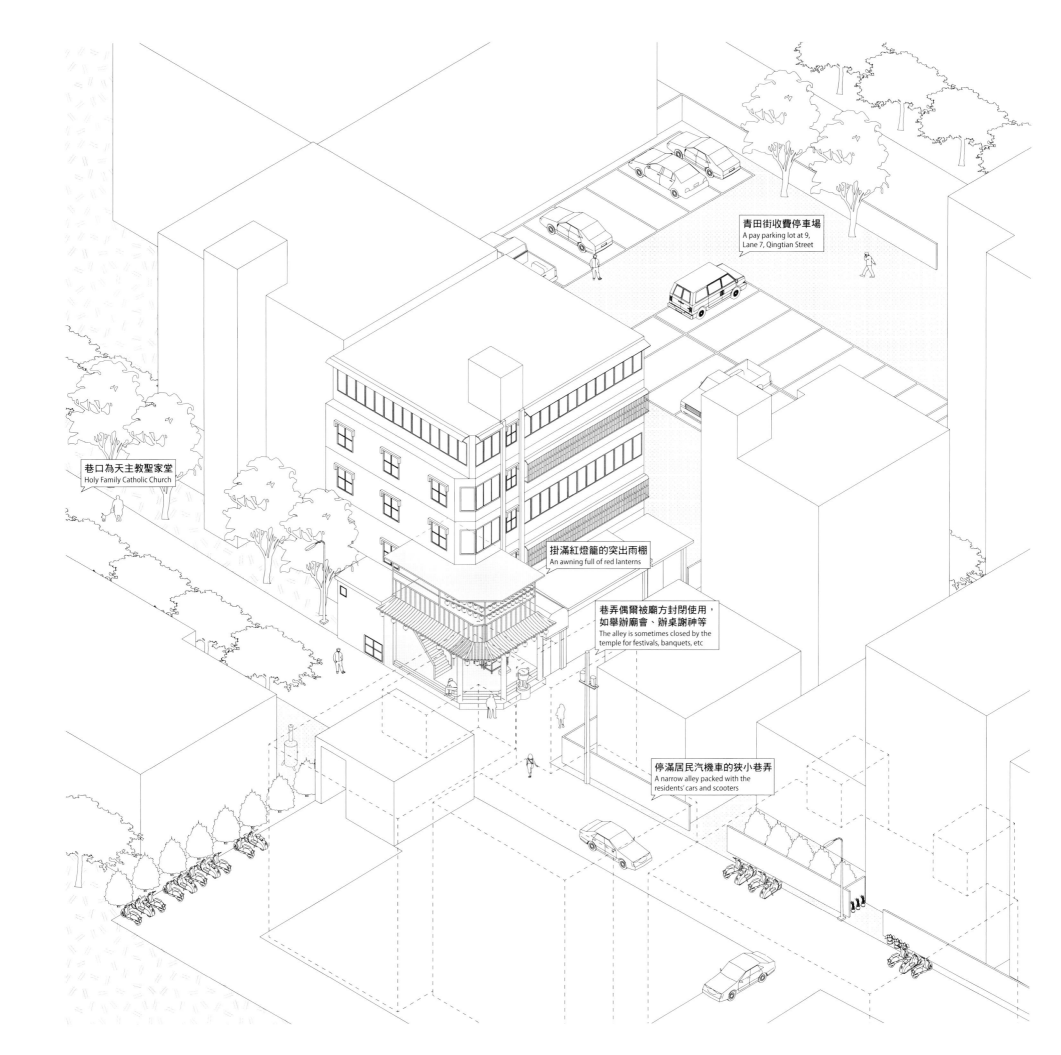

青田街收費停車場
A pay parking lot at 9, Lane 7, Qingtian Street

巷口為天主教聖家堂
Holy Family Catholic Church

掛滿紅燈籠的突出雨棚
An awning full of red lanterns

巷弄偶爾被廟方封閉使用，
如舉辦廟會、辦桌謝神等
The alley is sometimes closed by the temple for festivals, banquets, etc

停滿居民汽機車的狹小巷弄
A narrow alley packed with the residents' cars and scooters

17

室外梯廟
With Outdoor Stair Temple

台北士林奏天宮

25°5'58.3"N 121°31'35.9"E

L

士林區奏天宮在福林橋與外雙溪的河堤間的公寓三樓。因為所處位置十分醒目，福林橋又是天母與台北市的主要出入口，所以立面被拿來出租廣告，車來車往可看得到「給你一點顏色」的廣告標語。廣告看板下的外掛樓梯幾乎一樣醒目，因為奏天宮不像其他身處大樓、公寓裡面或頂樓的廟，是和公寓共用出入口，反而自己在公寓旁外加專用樓梯。

Zoutian Temple is on the third floor of an apartment across the Waishuang Creek levee near Fulin Bridge in Shilin District, Taipei. Fulin Bridge is the main route between Tianmu and downtown Taipei, which makes the spot of the temple so eye-catching that the side facing the river has a billboard for rent. The extra staircase under the billboard is almost equally attractive. Unlike other temples in an apartment building or on the top floor, Zoutian Temple has this extra staircase installed as its exclusive access.

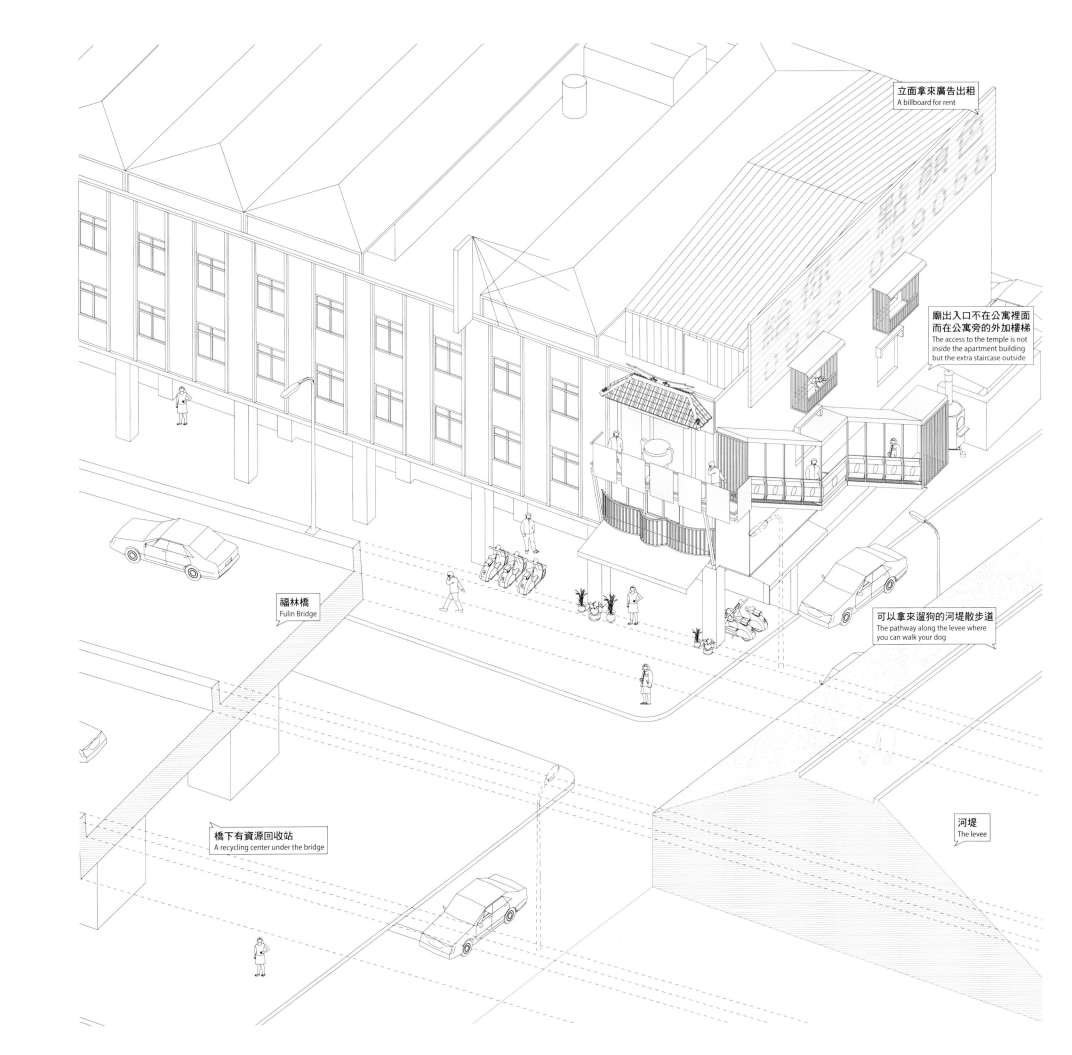

18

樓中廟
Apartment Temple

高雄左營文王宮

本廟位於高雄左營，屬於樓中廟系列，寄生於公寓住宅，卻僅外顯約 1 坪的都市空間。像是公寓住宅最常見的窗型冷氣的放大版，其建築外部附加物讓寄生特質格外明顯。在素來以違建、鐵窗文化為大眾所詬病的台灣都市中，本廟雖然並非建築師所設計，卻更加精準地融入台灣鐵窗文化的在地紋理，無疑是台灣五金業的傑作。

This temple in Zuoying, Kaohsiung, falls into the category of in-betweens. It resides in an apartment, and only exhibits itself within a frame of 3.31 square meters, which looks like an enlarged window type air conditioner commonly seen in apartment buildings. Cities in Taiwan are notorious for illegal buildings and iron window railing. This temple may not be designed by an architect, but it fits perfectly into the local architecture. It is definitely a work of the hardware industry in Taiwan.

22°41'12.6"N 120°18'15.8"E

典型台灣街屋社區與屋頂加建
Typical apartment buildings with add-ons on the rooftop

整個廟從立面看來就是超大的窗型冷氣
The temple looks like a giant window type air conditioner from outside

窗型冷氣
A window type air conditioner

典型台灣街屋住商混合下的一樓鐵捲門
An overhead door on the first floor of a building for both residential and commercial uses which is typical in Taiwan

19

屋頂廟
Roof Temple

台北松山李氏宗祠

李氏宗祠位於台北市松山區，與小巨蛋僅差一個街口的距離。宗祠可從一樓搭乘電梯抵達四五樓祭拜空間，中央自四樓往上挑高出三樓高的採光中庭，廟體往上加蓋出中式屋頂，看似頂樓加建的違建。在違建逐漸就地合法的台北城，李氏宗祠僅憑兩樓高的台廟立面語彙，就展現了台灣與西方都市的與眾不同。

The Ancestral Hall of the Lees is in downtown Taipei, just one block away from the Taipei Arena. The Hall on the fourth and fifth floors can be accessed by an elevator from the first floor. An atrium with a three-story-high ceiling is in the center of the fourth floor, with a Chinese-style rooftop covering the hall. It looks just like an illegal add-on. In the city of Taipei where more and more illegal buildings are made legal over time, the Ancestral Hall of the Lees, with its high-rise design, shows how different Taiwan cities and western cities are.

南京東路三段

敦化國中

25°3'7.2"N 121°32'49.1"E

L

在大樓裡的挑空空間與屋頂採光罩
An atrium and skylights

大樓裡很多整形診所
There are many plastic surgery clinics in the building

與大樓用戶共用的電梯
The elevator shared with the residents in the building

大樓入口也是宗祠入口
The gate to the building and the Hall as well

20

電話亭廟
Call Box Temple

台南永康菩薩堂

寄生廟發展至今或許可被歸類出不同的世代。在台南我們發現一座利用現有工業模組元件組構所形成的微型廟宇，該廟以電話亭為宿主，安然寄生於台19線上某座陸橋人行道上。

根據觀察，在非擁擠的都市空間中，多以建造大廟為首選。然而在預算及空間有限的條件下，寄生之廟藉由現成工業化產品即能擁有最簡便的廟體，並得以寄生在環境中任何我們隨處可見的角落。

Up until now, parasitic temples can be classified into different generations. In Tainan, we found a miniature temple built upon a ready-made industrial module. The temple takes a telephone booth as its host on a footbridge somewhere along Provincial Highway 19.

In uncrowded areas, building a grand temple is often the first choice. Due to budget and space limitations, however, a parasitic temple can obtain a simple body through a ready-made product of modern industry and find a host everywhere around us.

23°01'25"N 120°12'56.4"E

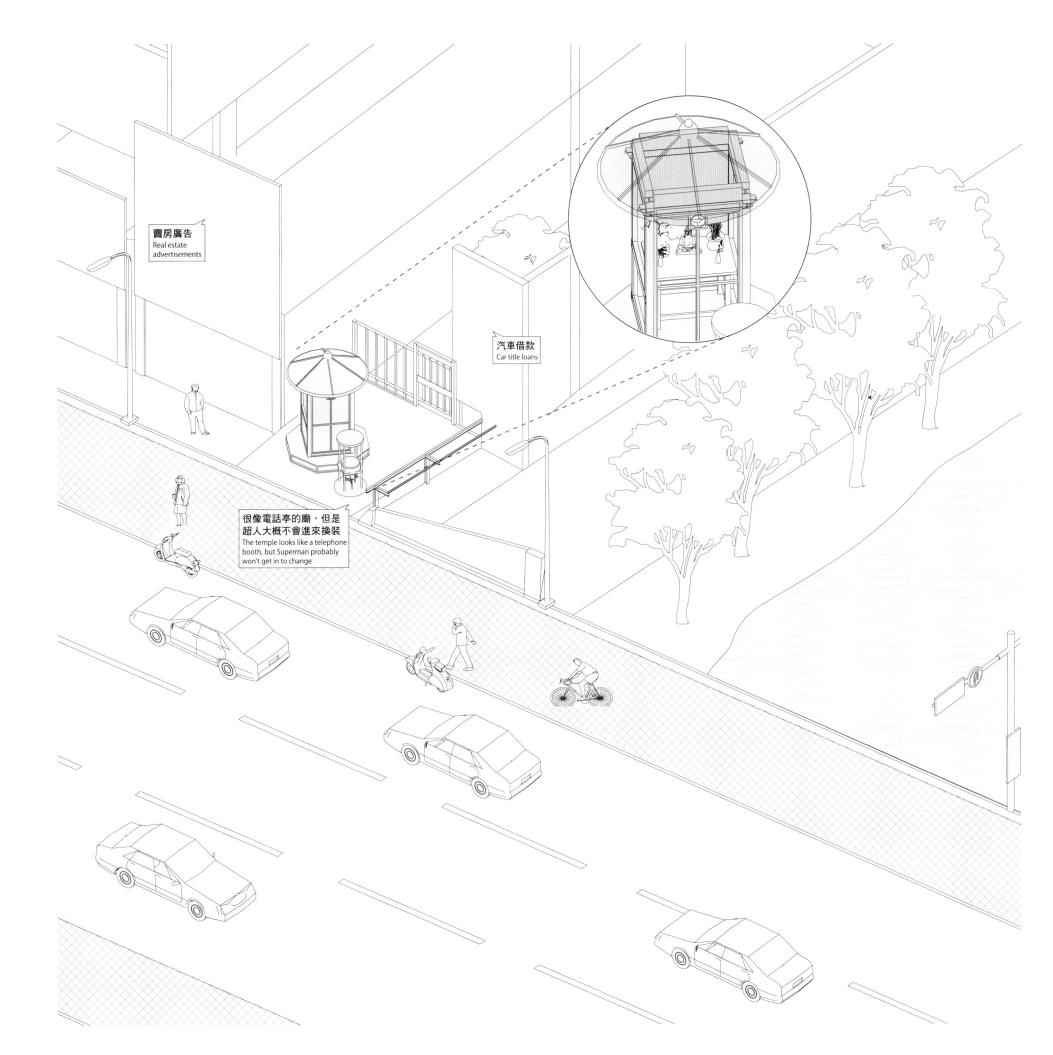

賣房廣告
Real estate
advertisements

汽車借款
Car title loans

很像電話亭的廟，但是
超人大概不會進來換裝
The temple looks like a telephone
booth, but Superman probably
won't get in to change

21

天橋下廟
Under Pedestrain Bridge Temple

台南莊敬福德正神

22°59'54.2"N 120°13'58.9"E

台南小東路電信局圍牆邊、人行陸橋大柱下寄生了一間土地公廟。據說廟址選地曾歷時多年、幾經波折，最後才於 2000 年在此地建廟落成。後來，有位來此參拜的通靈者發現這是一個非常好的風水地點，東南西北方鄰近的建築，以及廟後方那棵菩提樹，都具有風水上的象徵意義。

在台灣都市處處可見車行高架橋下的空間被作為各種用途使用，車行橋下的廟不是罕見的現象。然而人行陸橋下的廟卻很稀有，因其屋頂遮蔽的範圍，並不足以為廟的各類活動、提供遮風避雨的空間，上下橋的樓梯動線與廟幾乎緊貼，唯一解釋廟會出現這樣的選址，只有風水與民俗信仰上的原因。

Under a footbridge near a telecommunications facility of Chunghwa Telecom on Xiaodong Road, Tainan, a townsfolk found a great spot for a temple. Later, a psychic came to worship and said Fude Zhengshen ("Right God of Blessing and Virtue"), aka Tudigong, got enshrined at the right time, in the right place, and by the right people. He claimed that the bridge overhead was a living azure dragon, the sacred fig on the back was a parasol, the telecommunications building on the left was an official seal, the alley on the right was the Heaven's Gate, and the Liangmei Building was a vajra to strike demons.

In Taiwan, the space under an overpass is often used in various ways, and building a temple there is one of them. A temple under a footbridge and next to the staircase, however, is not so common because it is not wide enough to shelter all ritual ceremonies. The only explanation of the location choice is fengshui and folk belief.

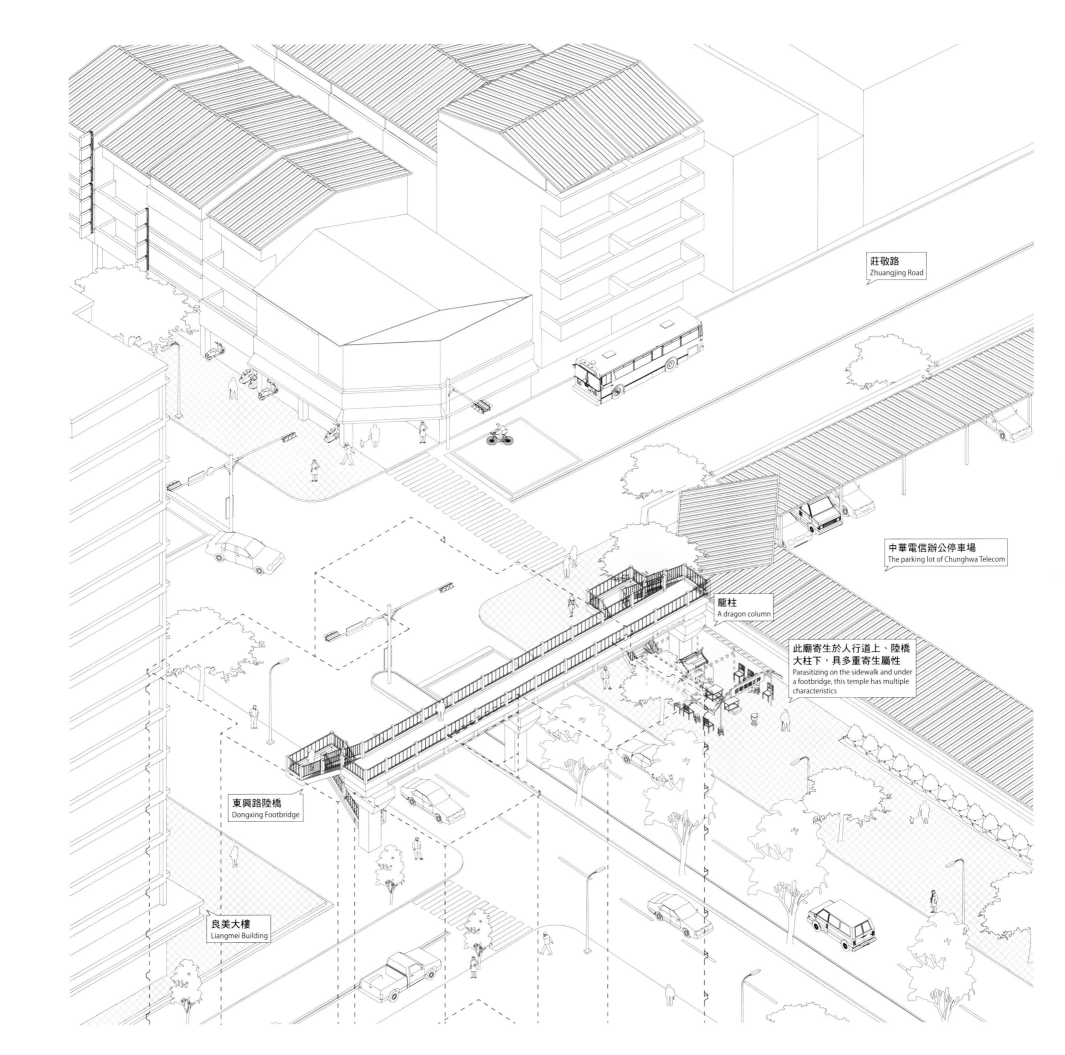

莊敬路
Zhuangjing Road

中華電信辦公停車場
The parking lot of Chunghwa Telecom

龍柱
A dragon column

此廟寄生於人行道上、陸橋
大柱下，具多重寄生屬性
Parasitizing on the sidewalk and under
a footbridge, this temple has multiple
characteristics

東興路陸橋
Dongxing Footbridge

良美大樓
Liangmei Building

22

寵物屋廟
Pet House Temple

台北木柵萬聖公廟

24°59'34"N 121°34'16.6"E

XXS

台北木柵路四段的寵物屋廟萬聖公，見證了台灣五金業的發達與廟的工業化。與其說它是一個建築廟，倒不如說它是一個產品廟，一個工廠預組好的金屬狗屋改裝成廟更貼切，一個買了就可以落地安裝在人行道上的廟，就位在「名人山莊」社區圍牆與人行道擋土牆夾出的凹角中。也許是因為靈驗，廟上方掛滿了信徒還願的布條「有求必應」。

Wanshenggong, enshrined in a pet house temple at Section 4, Muzha Road, witnesses the achievement of Taiwan's hardware industry and industrialization of temples. Rather than a temple built, it is more suitable to call it a temple produced, a temple modified from a preassembled metal dog house, which could be "bought" and instantly installed on the sidewalk. Currently it is on the corner of a retaining wall on the sidewalk and the wall of a nearby community, Celebrity Villas. There are many banners saying "Totally Responsive, Completely Efficacious" hung in the temple, which are gifts from grateful devotees who got their wishes come true.

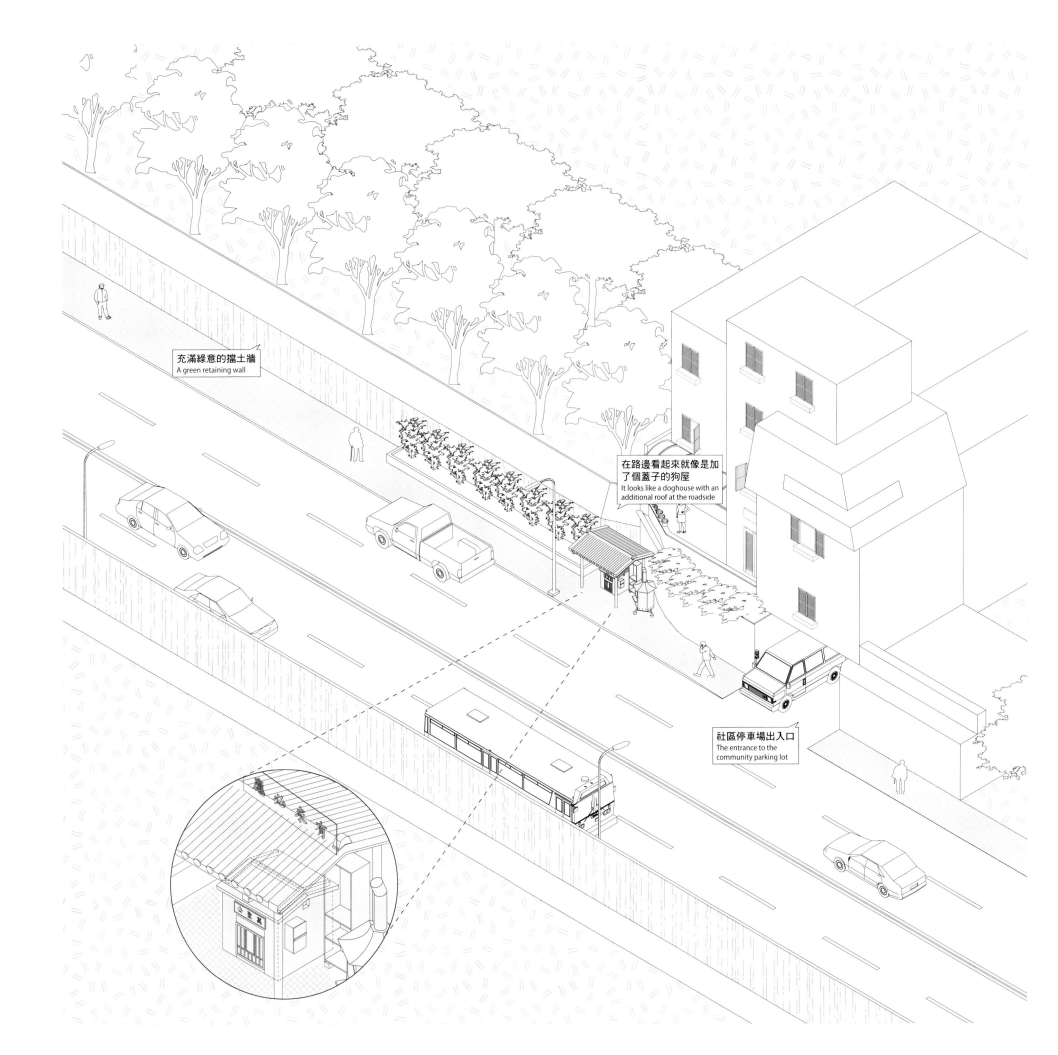

充滿綠意的擋土牆
A green retaining wall

在路邊看起來就像是加了個蓋子的狗屋
It looks like a doghouse with an additional roof at the roadside

社區停車場出入口
The entrance to the community parking lot

23

圓環廟
Roundabout
Temple

台中大坑福德祠

24°10'44.5"N 120°44'23.9"E

大坑圓環土地公廟現址會建造圓環，不是因為交通規劃需要圓環調整車流方向，而是神明的意思。從日治時期開始，因為圓環這棵老楓香，這裡成為大坑的地標，最早一開始只放了三顆石頭就充當廟了，直到 1962 年才由居民共同集資建廟。而後為了都市發展進行道路規劃時，因為神明不想搬走，便將廟保留在圓環裡，道路從旁繞過。

Tudigong Temple at the roundabout has a very long history. During Japanese rule, three rocks were piled beside an old Formosan gum, the landmark of Dakeng, to represent Tudigong for people to worship and pray.

In 1962, the residents raised money to rebuild the temple with brick to enshrine both Tudigong and his wife, Tudipo. Later when the government was planning urban traffic, the temple was preserved and roads had to go around it.

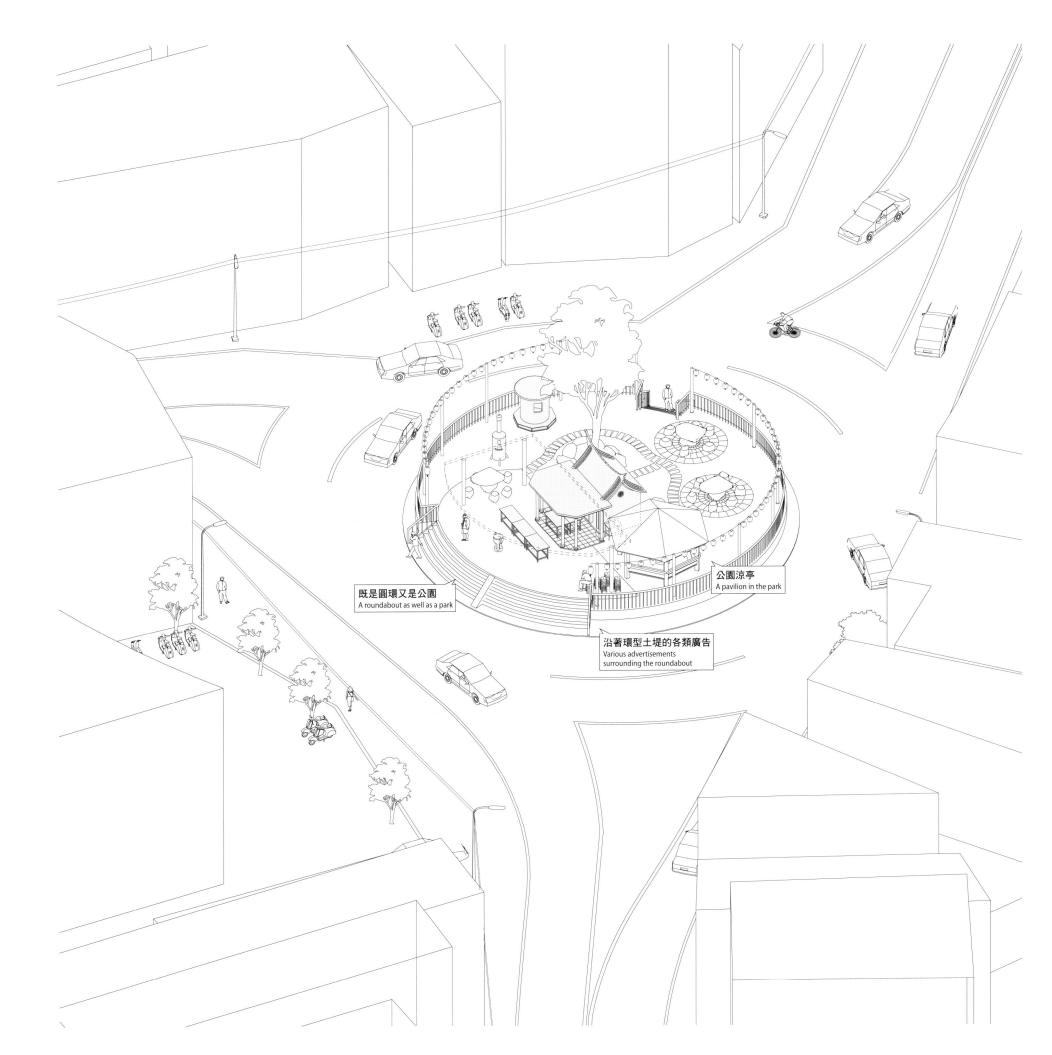

既是圓環又是公園
A roundabout as well as a park

公園涼亭
A pavilion in the park

沿著環型土堤的各類廣告
Various advertisements
surrounding the roundabout

24

路上廟
Traffic Island Temple

新北石碇八分寮福德宮

新北市石碇區北深路與楓林橋的交叉口上有一座突出路面的分隔島——石碇福德宮。旁邊和平國小的學生上課路上都會看到它。過去，有專屬的人行天橋可直接跨越車道走到安全島上的廟中；天橋拆除後，安全島上的廟也進行改建，改變了廟的位置。現在只能拾階登上嵌在安全島中的樓梯到達這個地面島上的廟。

Fude Temple of Bafenliao, Shiding, is located at the intersection of Beishen Road and famous Fenglin Bridge, only a bicycle lane away from Heping Elementary School on the hill. It is interesting that there used to be a footbridge for the exclusive use of people who wanted to cross the roads and get to the temple. After the footbridge was removed, the temple was modified as well. Now devotees can only get to the elevated temple through a new staircase embedded in the traffic island.

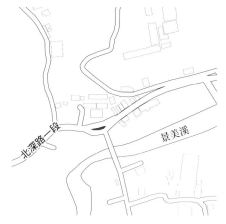

25°00'40.3"N 121°38'30.0"E

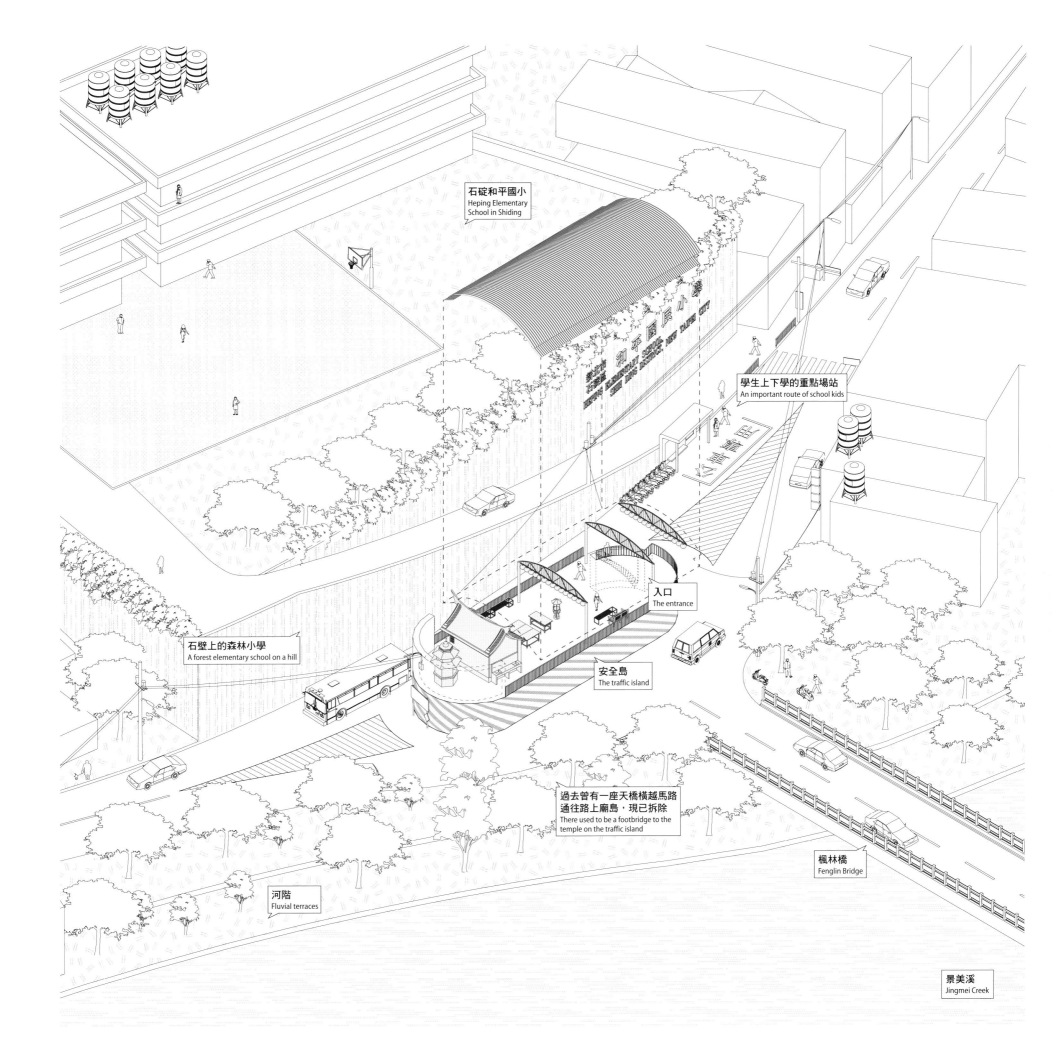

石碇和平國小
Heping Elementary
School in Shiding

學生上下學的重點場站
An important route of school kids

入口
The entrance

石壁上的森林小學
A forest elementary school on a hill

安全島
The traffic island

過去曾有一座天橋橫越馬路
通往路上廟島，現已拆除
There used to be a footbridge to the
temple on the traffic island

楓林橋
Fenglin Bridge

河階
Fluvial terraces

景美溪
Jingmei Creek

25

地下廟
Underground Temple

台北木柵風動石聖公

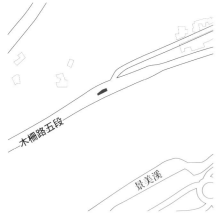

25°0'7.54"N 121°34'52.4"E

台北文山區的風動石聖公源自台灣常見的自然崇拜。初始時因風動、石落所建，1986 年道路拓寬，石聖公顯靈使工程單位無法移廟，從此路面墊高，形成目前我們所蒐集到、唯一位於地下（路面之下）的寄生廟。

路中廟的建造大多起因於事故頻傳或無法搬遷，風動石聖公卻因位於地下，其舊有的廟體屋頂阻擋行車視線而造成該路段事故頻傳，故過去此廟位於地面上的違建部分，近年來已被拆除。而拆除之後留下的三個地表上的三個空洞（其中兩個是樓梯間）形成了三個採光井，其錯落的幾何圖案令人不禁聯想到安藤忠雄在直島的地中美術館。拆除違建讓風動石聖公往下一步演化成如地下展場般的「台灣都市廟版的地中美術館」。

The belief in Fengdong Shishenggong ("Lord of the Balanced Rock") in Wenshan District, Taipei, originated from nature worship which is common in Taiwan. The temple was built after the rocks fell from the hill and balanced itself even when the wind rocked it. When the road was to be broadened and road level to be raised in 1986, the government decided to destroy the temple. Excavators, however, were out of order one by one for no apparent reason. Rumor had it that it was Lord of the Balanced Rock who caused the heavy construction equipment to malfunction. Afterwards, the administration canceled the destruction and continued the road construction by bypassing the temple. Hence, the only underground parasitic temple we have gathered so far was formed.

Most of the road temples are formed because of strange events (like the above) or difficulty in moving. Since Fengdong Shishenggong went underground, its old rooftop, which blocked drivers' sight, had caused many accidents. Therefore, some of its upper parts have been removed, leaving three skylight shafts (two of them are stairwells). Its geometry reminds people of the Chichu Art Museum in the island of Naoshima in Kagawa Prefecture, Japan, designed by architect Tadao Anto. Maybe it is a good way for the temple to show itself.

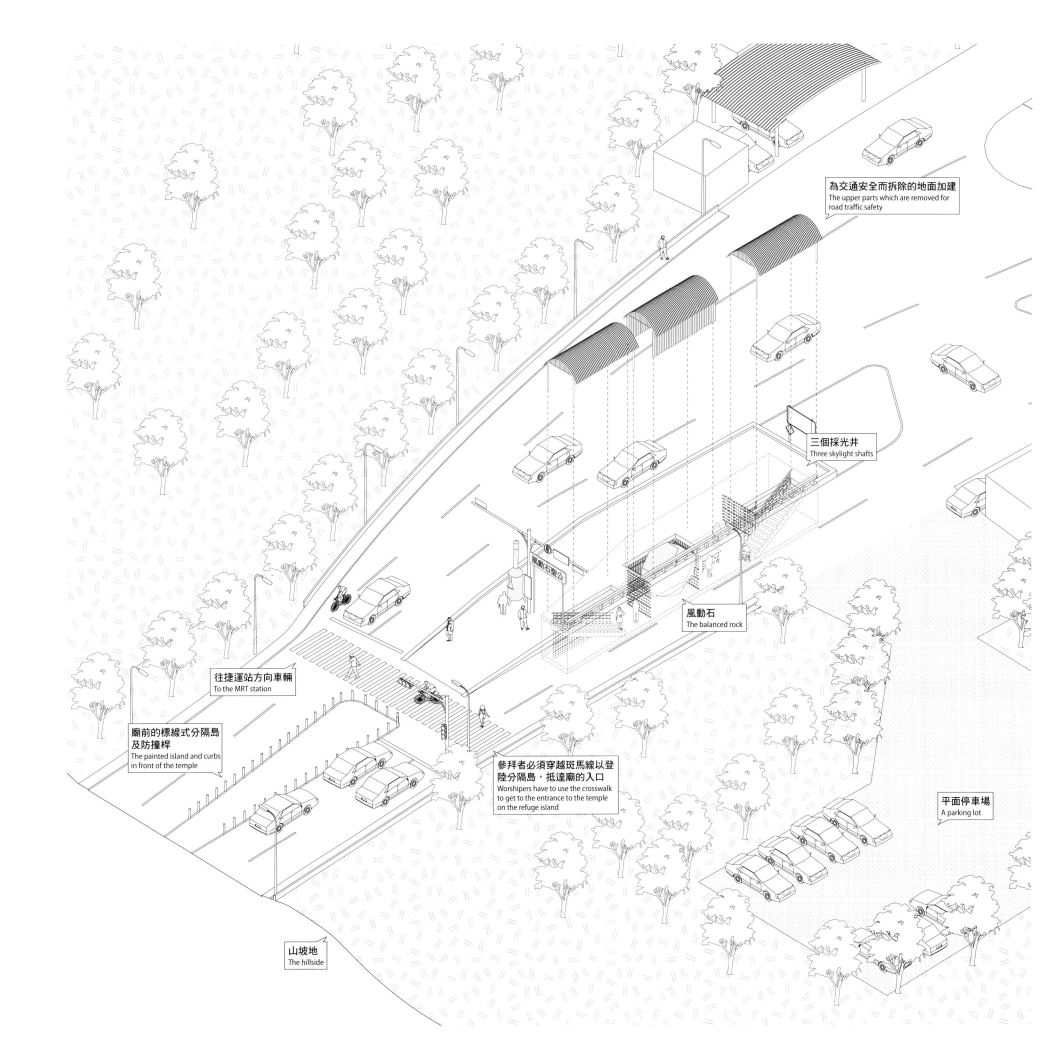

為交通安全而拆除的地面加建
The upper parts which are removed for
road traffic safety

三個採光井
Three skylight shafts

風動石
The balanced rock

往捷運站方向車輛
To the MRT station

廟前的標線式分隔島
及防撞桿
The painted island and curbs
in front of the temple

參拜者必須穿越斑馬線以登
陸分隔島，抵達廟的入口
Worshipers have to use the crosswalk
to get to the entrance to the temple
on the refuge island

平面停車場
A parking lot

山坡地
The hillside

26

貼牆廟
Infrastructure Temple

台北萬華水濂宮

環河快速道路

桂林路

25°2'25.3"N 121°29'52.4"E

2010年7月，我於一次活動中發現此廟，從此開始有「寄生之廟」的構想。

萬華水濂宮作為第一個引人注意的寄生之廟，在於它位於城市的邊界與基礎設施交會的地帶，廟體與義警協勤中心相鄰，走進廟裡才發現，其退縮出一個極窄的走道空間，並與義警協勤中心後門相通，連同以五金行為主的商街，皆位在環河南路橋下的人行道上。加上廟體看似與環河快速道路下的河堤設施共用壁體，可解讀成不只一個宿主。從發現第一個寄生之廟時，就同步衍生出「多重寄生」這個用來記錄寄生廟時所用的屬性。

In July 2010, the idea of "parasitic temples" struck me when I discovered this temple in an event.

As parasitic temple number one, Shuilian Temple ("Water Curtain Temple") in Wanhua attracts people for its location in the joint of the city boarder and a public infrastructure. The temple is adjacent to the Volunteer Police Command Center. There is a slim sidewalk outside the temple which leads to the back door to the Command Center and other hardware stores on the street. It looks like that the body of the temple shares the wall with the levee under New Taipei Huanhe Expressway; hence it can be interpreted as having two hosts for one temple. Since the first parasitic temple was discovered, the term "multiple parasitic" has been attributed to it.

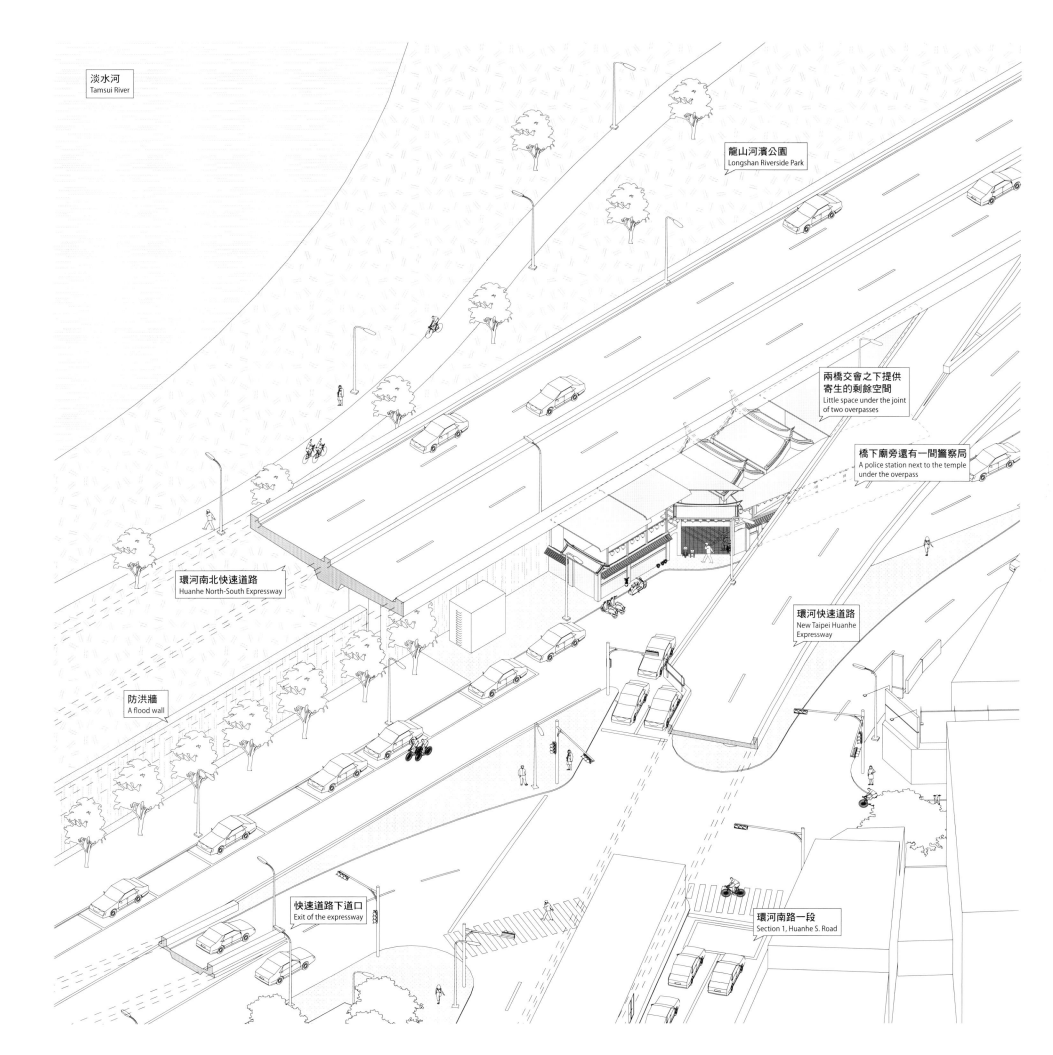

淡水河
Tamsui River

龍山河濱公園
Longshan Riverside Park

兩橋交會之下提供
寄生的剩餘空間
Little space under the joint
of two overpasses

橋下廟旁還有一間警察局
A police station next to the temple
under the overpass

環河南北快速道路
Huanhe North-South Expressway

環河快速道路
New Taipei Huanhe
Expressway

防洪牆
A flood wall

快速道路下道口
Exit of the expressway

環河南路一段
Section 1, Huanhe S. Road

27
一坡三廟
Triple Temples on a Hillside

台北中正福佛宮

25°01'14.9"N 121°31'08.5"E

台北中正區牯嶺街附近的河堤外面有一特殊寄生廟群——一坡三廟，這個名字源自三廟聚集的特性。三間廟宇共用同一個出入口，距離極近卻擁有各自的主神。由於三廟都位於河堤的最下層，廟埕空間也隨著河道間歇性的沖積狀況而時大時小。

一坡三廟並非單一的廟的群聚現象，我們尚能夠見到一樹三廟或一集合社區三廟或多廟的狀態。

而這正說明了台灣宗教與民間信仰具有相當的包容性，這些廟得以寄生在同一塊基地上。即便因為不同的信仰及需求而建，這些廟宇，仍舊共同庇佑偶然造訪、發現並誠心參拜的廣大信眾。

The name "Triple Temples on a Hillside" describes a cluster of three temples. The three temples, which are extremely close to one another, share one gateway, but each of them has its own main deity. The three temples are all at the lowest level outside the levee, so the area of their squares vary depending on the intermittent flow to the alluvium.

Triple Temples on a Hillside is not a unique case of a temple cluster. We can also find triple temples under a tree, triple temples within a community, or even more multiple temples in one spot.

This illustrates the very tolerance and inclusiveness of religion and folk beliefs in Taiwan. These temples, though built for different beliefs and needs, take host on the same piece of land, all blessing the occasional yet devoted worshippers.

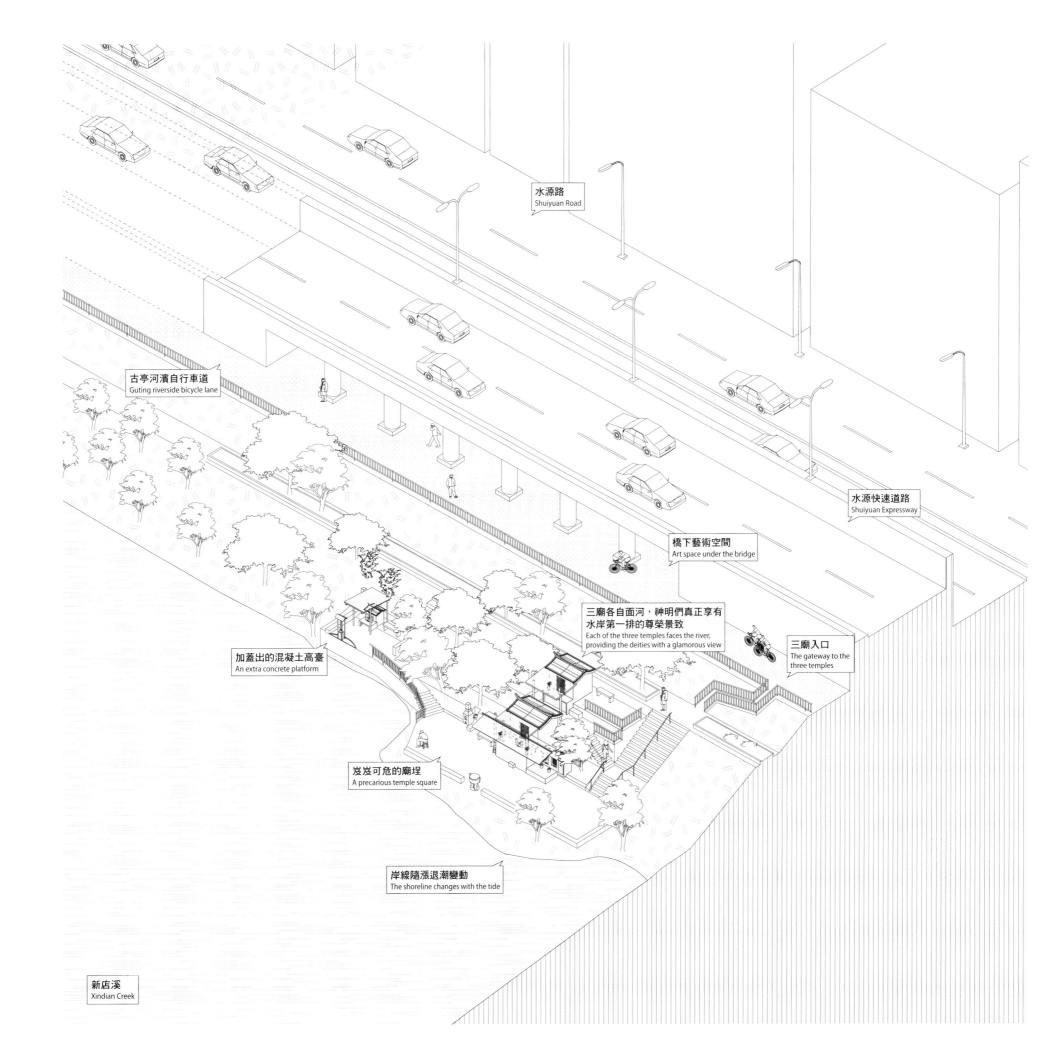

水源路
Shuiyuan Road

古亭河濱自行車道
Guting riverside bicycle lane

水源快速道路
Shuiyuan Expressway

橋下藝術空間
Art space under the bridge

三廟各自面河，神明們真正享有
水岸第一排的尊榮景致
Each of the three temples faces the river,
providing the deities with a glamorous view

三廟入口
The gateway to the three temples

加蓋出的混凝土高臺
An extra concrete platform

岌岌可危的廟埕
A precarious temple square

岸線隨漲退潮變動
The shoreline changes with the tide

新店溪
Xindian Creek

28

升降廟
Lift Temple

台北士林天德宮

台北劍潭抽水站、三腳渡碼頭旁有間天德宮，它寄生於河堤位置的最下層，卻有全台灣獨一無二的升降裝置，在面對大雨洪患時能舉起自己。為多尊落難神明而建的天德宮，全廟以鐵板製成，重達14噸，最高可升至7M高的堤頂高度。此廟充分反映出台灣人在面對洪患的壓力下，所展現的驚人創意。

Tiande Temple, located near Jiantan Pumping Station and Sanjiaodu Ferry Port, parasitizes in the lowest level outside the levee. It owns a one-of-a-kind elevating device which can lift the temple when the river is in flood. The main deity of the temple is Tudigong, but it also takes in all kinds of stray deities. Built with iron plate, Tiande Temple weighs 14 tons and can be elevated up to as high as the nearby levee at 7 meters. This temple reflects the amazing creativity of the Taiwanese when facing the threat of the flood.

25°04'51.8"N 121°31'03.0"E

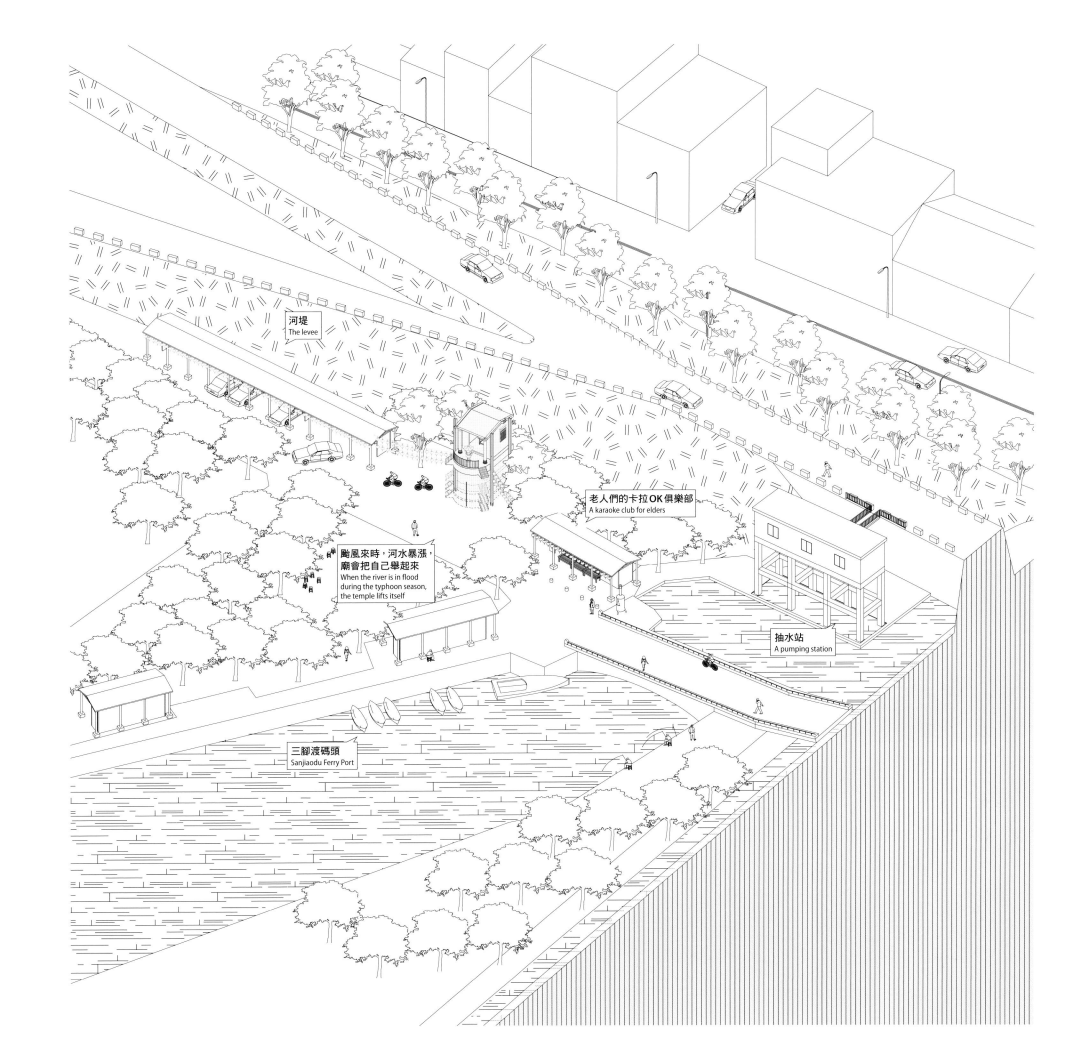

河堤
The levee

老人們的卡拉OK俱樂部
A karaoke club for elders

颱風來時，河水暴漲，廟會把自己舉起來
When the river is in flood during the typhoon season, the temple lifts itself

抽水站
A pumping station

三腳渡碼頭
Sanjiaodu Ferry Port

29

擋土牆廟
Retaining Wall Temple

台北南港善南宮

25°2'59.1"N 121°36'56.0"E

善南宮位於南港研究院路一段130號。二戰末期，一棵距今約110年的茄苳樹顯神蹟因而建廟。廟體建於擋土牆上，從側梯往上先看見茄苳公，再往上走才為主廟與一個空中的廟埕，一個算得上是開放空間的地方。從擋土牆本身可以看出不同的建造時間。自茄苳公開始建造自己的擋土牆，後來善南宮再往上堆疊、建立自己的擋土設施。形成一個擋土牆上出現兩廟，且與樹一體的特殊案例。

環境的轉變，帶動著廟與都市的寄生關係。而依循不同的建造年代、材料工法與寄生方式，寄生廟即使可被分類，但仍然獨一無二。

Shannan Temple is near a 110-year-old autumn maple tree at 130, Section 1, Academia Road, Nangang District, Taipei. It is said that when Allied forces bombed Nangang during the last stages of the Second World War, the tree revealed the shape of a Buddha after being hit by a shell. Later, the villagers built the temple to thank the Lord of the Tree. The temple is adjacent to a retaining wall. Climbing the stairs, you can see the enshrined Lord of the Tree first, and then the primary temple and a quite open square upstairs. From the retaining wall, we can recognize the stages of construction. The retaining wall was built for the Lord of the Tree first, and then Shannan Temple was added upon it with more retaining facilities. Now we have a special case of double temples on a retaining wall with a tree.

Environmental changes affect the parasitic relationship between temples and cities. Although parasitic temples can be categorized according to the time, material, methods of construction and parasitic ways, each one of them is still one of a kind.

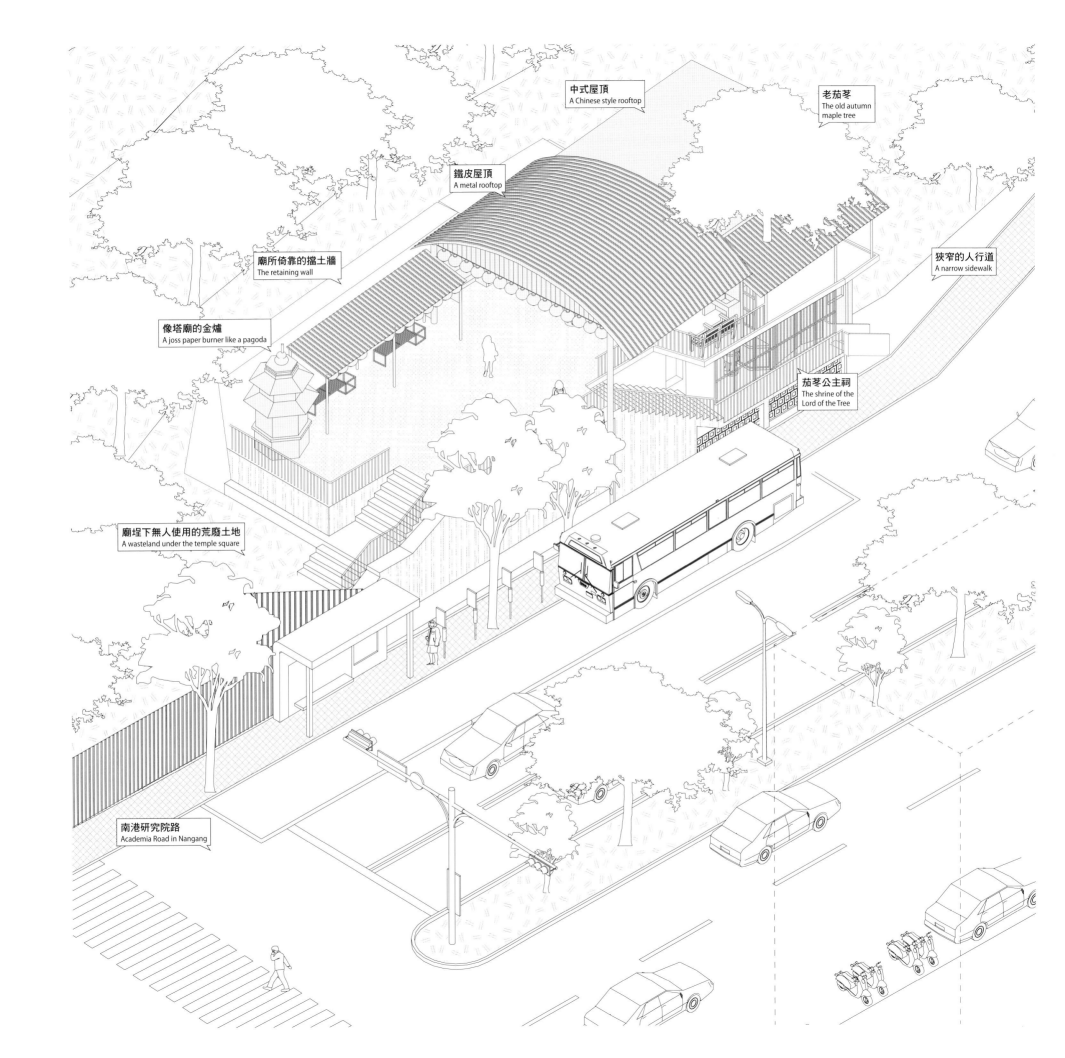

中式屋頂
A Chinese style rooftop

老茄苳
The old autumn maple tree

鐵皮屋頂
A metal rooftop

廟所倚靠的擋土牆
The retaining wall

狹窄的人行道
A narrow sidewalk

像塔廟的金爐
A joss paper burner like a pagoda

茄苳公主祠
The shrine of the Lord of the Tree

廟埕下無人使用的荒廢土地
A wasteland under the temple square

南港研究院路
Academia Road in Nangang

30

橋下廟
Under Bridge Temple

台北士林文昌堂

25°5'52.2"N 121°31'13.8"E

橋下廟位於士林區文昌橋下，北堤外為外雙溪，橋的兩側滿是傳統公寓住宅，而文昌堂就在這都市的隙縫下，找到一絲生存的空間。

　　這座寄生於橋下的廟，面臨橋下的雙向道路與周邊非垂直正的街道。其橋下空間十分壓迫，自人行道到橋梁只有2.3~2.6M的高度。與文昌堂一起寄生於文昌橋橋下的，還有社區居民的活動中心與資源回收站，三者形成一個共生在橋下的綜合體。

Wenchang Temple is under Wenchang Bridge in Shilin District. To the north, there is Waishuang Creek over the levee. Around both sides of the bridge crowd old apartment buildings. It is in this tiny gap in the city that Wenchang Temple found its place to survive.

　　This temple, parasitizing under a bridge, faces a two-way road which is surrounded by many irregular blocks. The height between the sidewalk and the bridge is only 2.3 to 2.6 meters, making people cramped. Alongside Wenchang Temple under Wenchang Bridge are community and recycling centers. The three of them make a symbiotic flock under the bridge.

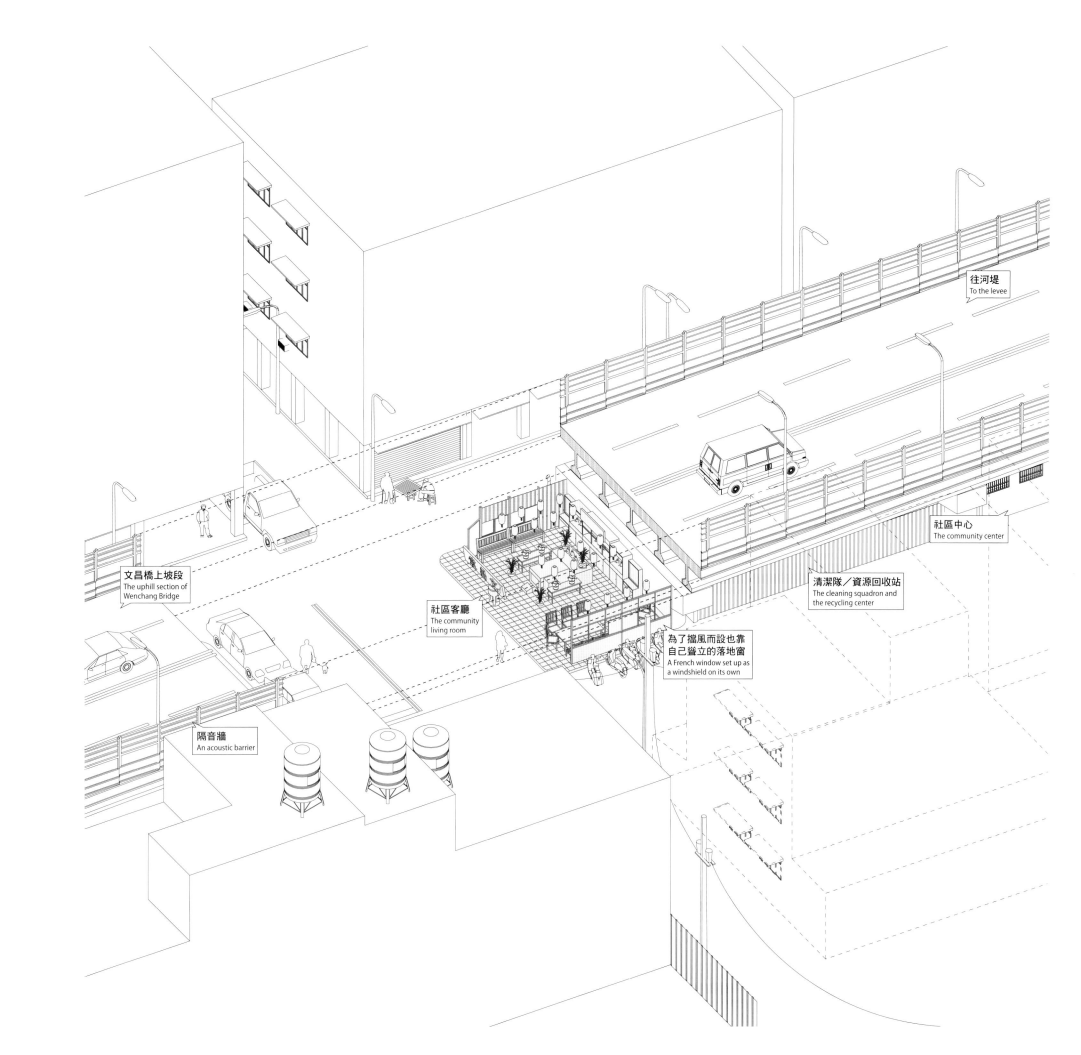

往河堤
To the levee

社區中心
The community center

文昌橋上坡段
The uphill section of
Wenchang Bridge

社區客廳
The community
living room

清潔隊／資源回收站
The cleaning squadron and
the recycling center

為了擋風而設也靠
自己聳立的落地窗
A French window set up as
a windshield on its own

隔音牆
An acoustic barrier

31

橋下廟群
Under Bridge
Temples

台北萬華福德宮、奉天宮等

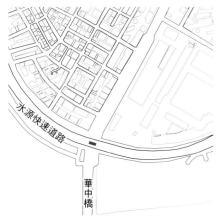

25°0'59.4"N 121°29'44.2"E

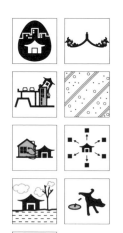

M

華中橋南北向連接台北市萬華區及新北市永和區，東西向的水源快速道路橫跨華中橋，在這兩座橋交會的地面層，提供了廟宇寄生、四面被道路分隔的分隔島空間。在這個分隔島區共有三間廟宇：福德宮、奉天宮及不知名的小廟，供奉著不同的主神。主要的福德宮背對河濱公園水門，正門面向五線道。分隔島之大，廟體、廟埕、流動廁所及小型機車停放區一應俱全，只是使用者必須從四面穿越車速極快的道路，才能驚險抵達。在尖峰時刻，果菜市場的活動也拓展到這五線道以及周邊的停車場上，攤販們沿著分隔島就地擺放貨品進行買賣交易。鄰近的高樓住宅雖然標誌了「面水第一排」的優越區位，但整個環境卻更像是台北市的邊陲地帶。處在市場的髒亂以及被四向車道分隔的孤島，廟群就這樣寄生在長時間被四面橋體四面包圍而產生的陰影之中，略顯陰暗。

While meridional Huazhong Bridge connects Wanhua District of Taipei and Yonhe District of New Taipei, elevated zonal Shuiyuan Expressway spans the bridge. On the ground level beneath the joint of the two overpasses, there is a traffic island surrounded by four roads. It is within this bizarre block that three temples find their place, each of which enshrining a different deity. The main temple, Fude Temple, faces a five-lane road with a floodgate to the riverside park behind it. The island is so spacious that it accommodates the temple body, the temple square, portable toilets, and a scooter parking lot. The downside of it is that people have to cross busy roads with speedy traffic, which is quite dangerous. During rush hours, activities of the fruit and vegetable market expand to the five-lane road and the nearby parking lot. Vendors along the island spread their goods on the ground for sale. The neighboring residential buildings boast of their superior position as "being at the first row to the river," but the local environment makes it more like the borderland of Taipei. Isolated on the island surrounded by filth of the market and heavy traffic, this cluster of temples parasitizes in the shadow and looks quite gloomy.

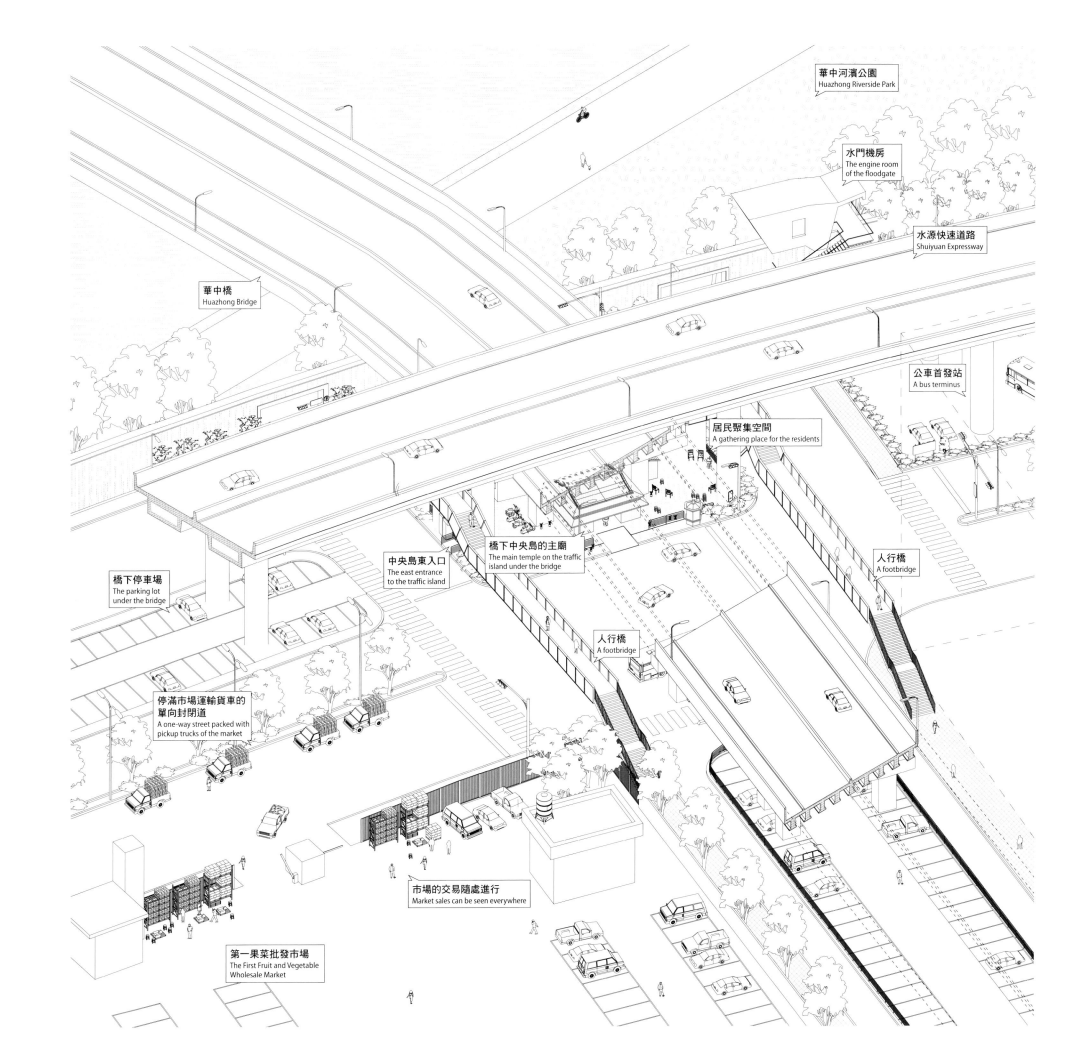

華中河濱公園
Huazhong Riverside Park

水門機房
The engine room of the floodgate

水源快速道路
Shuiyuan Expressway

華中橋
Huazhong Bridge

公車首發站
A bus terminus

居民聚集空間
A gathering place for the residents

中央島東入口
The east entrance to the traffic island

橋下中央島的主廟
The main temple on the traffic island under the bridge

人行橋
A footbridge

橋下停車場
The parking lot under the bridge

人行橋
A footbridge

停滿市場運輸貨車的單向封閉道
A one-way street packed with pickup trucks of the market

市場的交易隨處進行
Market sales can be seen everywhere

第一果菜批發市場
The First Fruit and Vegetable Wholesale Market

32

畸零地廟
Sidewalk Extrusion Temple

台北中山生福祠

25°03'53.4"N 121°31'37.6"E

生福祠位在中山區農安街與新生北路口，除了主祀土地公，還祭祀地府陰公。從神像、牌位以及位於奇特的位置上來看，推測早期應是先有生福祠，周邊的農田隨著後來的都市開發，原本的農耕景象被現在的高樓大廈和汽車所取代。許多類似此種比周邊紋理更早形成的廟宇，在後來的都市計畫下仍得以保存。姑且不論當時的都市計畫落實的法令、設計或執行等層面與西方主流都市規劃是否能齊平並論，但就文化保存與對既有紋理的退讓尊重，放之於現今社會，仍值得我們借鏡。

Located on the corner of Non'an Street and Xinsheng North Road in Zhongshan District, Shengfu Hall enshrines not only Tudigong but also Difu Yingong, "stray ghosts." Judging from the idol, spirit tablets, and its bizarre location, the hall was built first in early times. As the farmland disappeared during urban development, the farming landscape was replaced by high-rises and cars. Many of this kind of temple which appeared earlier than its surrounding buildings or facilities are preserved in urban planning. Whether the regulations or design or practice of the urban planning then was on a par with that of the western world, its cultural preservation and respect for the past, until now, are still worthy of reference.

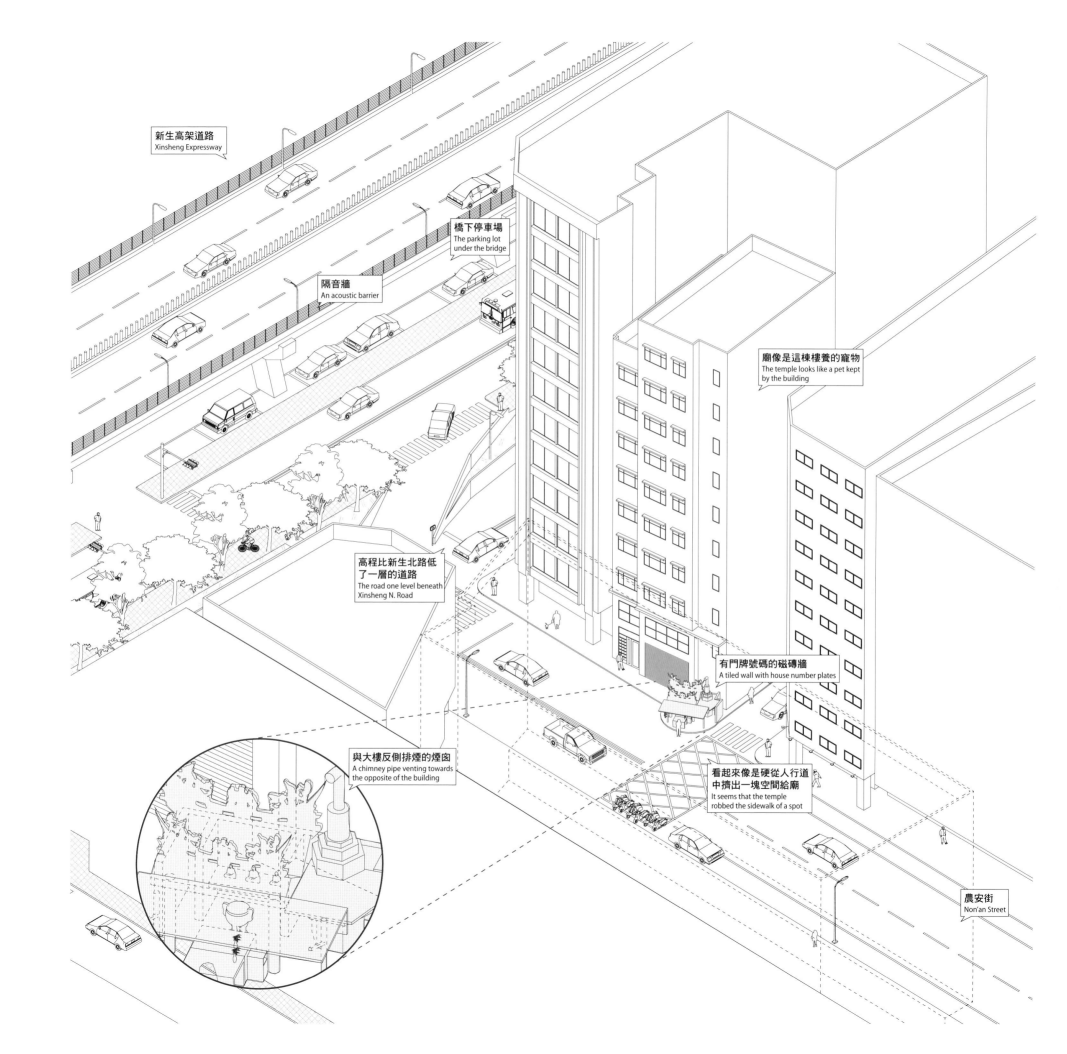

33

夾縫廟
Gap Temple

台北北投育仁福德宮

育仁福德宮位於捷運北投站北方的育仁路上，斜對三岔路口。廟宇本身一層高，有牌樓及雨棚，立地於臨棟住商混合的建築物夾縫間。牌樓及金爐位於人行道上，雨棚接續並連結臨棟建築的雨遮，形成類似騎樓的空間。廟方會參與每年農曆的一月十一號的「北投大拜拜」（北投慈后宮）年度遶境活動。

Yuren Fude Temple is on Yuren Street, north to the Taipei Metro Beitou Station, near a three-way junction. The temple is one story high and has a pailou and an awning. The pailou and the joss paper burner are on the sidewalk. The awning are connected to that of the adjacent building, making it look like a qilou. The temple participates in the annual pilgrimage activity of Cihou Temple of Beitou on the eleventh day of the first lunar month.

25°7'59.3"N 121°29'53.7"E

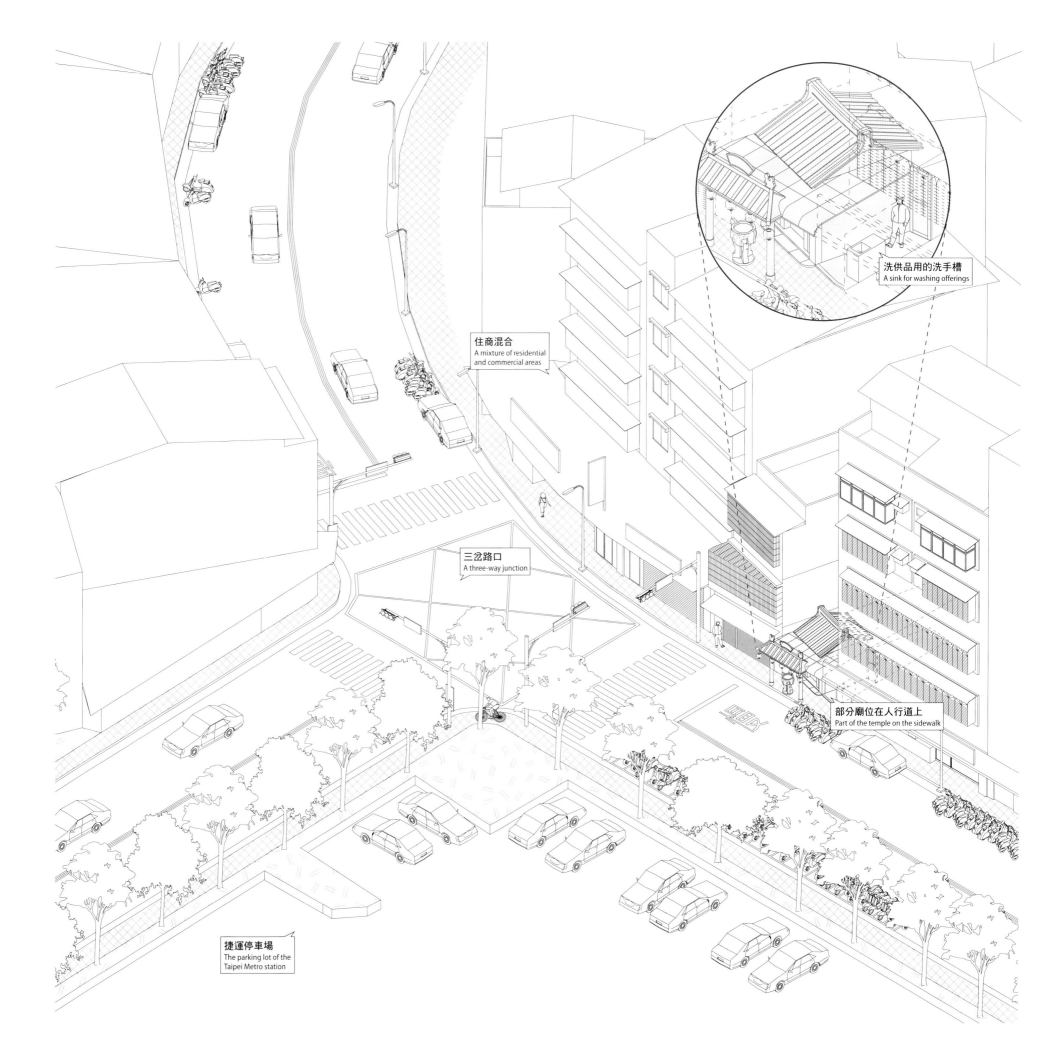

洗供品用的洗手槽
A sink for washing offerings

住商混合
A mixture of residential
and commercial areas

三岔路口
A three-way junction

部分廟位在人行道上
Part of the temple on the sidewalk

捷運停車場
The parking lot of the
Taipei Metro station

34

公園廟
Park Temple

台北松山敦中公園應媽廟

25°3'0.2"N 121°32'44.8"E

XXS

松山應媽廟位於四周都是住宅區的敦中公園之中。背對公園中心，以公園轉角廣場為廟埕與敦化國中南側圍牆隔街對望。應媽廟旁有運動設施、兒童遊樂場、涼亭、座椅、大量的綠蔭與櫻花，是周遭社區里民交誼、運動的場所。平日下午，老人家們喜歡在公園中應媽廟四周的座椅泡茶聊天，一旁的看護也會聚集交流。到了傍晚，會有家長帶小朋友到公園嬉戲。特殊活動時，甚至會在廟前掛起紅燈籠作為「光明燈」祈求應媽的保佑。

Songshan Yingma Temple is in Dunzhong Park, surrounded by residential areas. The center of the park is behind the temple, and the corner of the park is used as the temple square, facing the south wall of Dunhua Junior High School. There are sports facilities, a playground, a pavilion, benches, plenty of trees and even cherry blossoms around the temple, a place where villagers gather and exercise. In the afternoon, the elders like to make teas and chat on the benches around the temple, and their caretakers also get into groups. In the evening, parents bring their children to play in the park. On special occasions, red lanterns will be hung in front the temple as worship candles to pray to the deity.

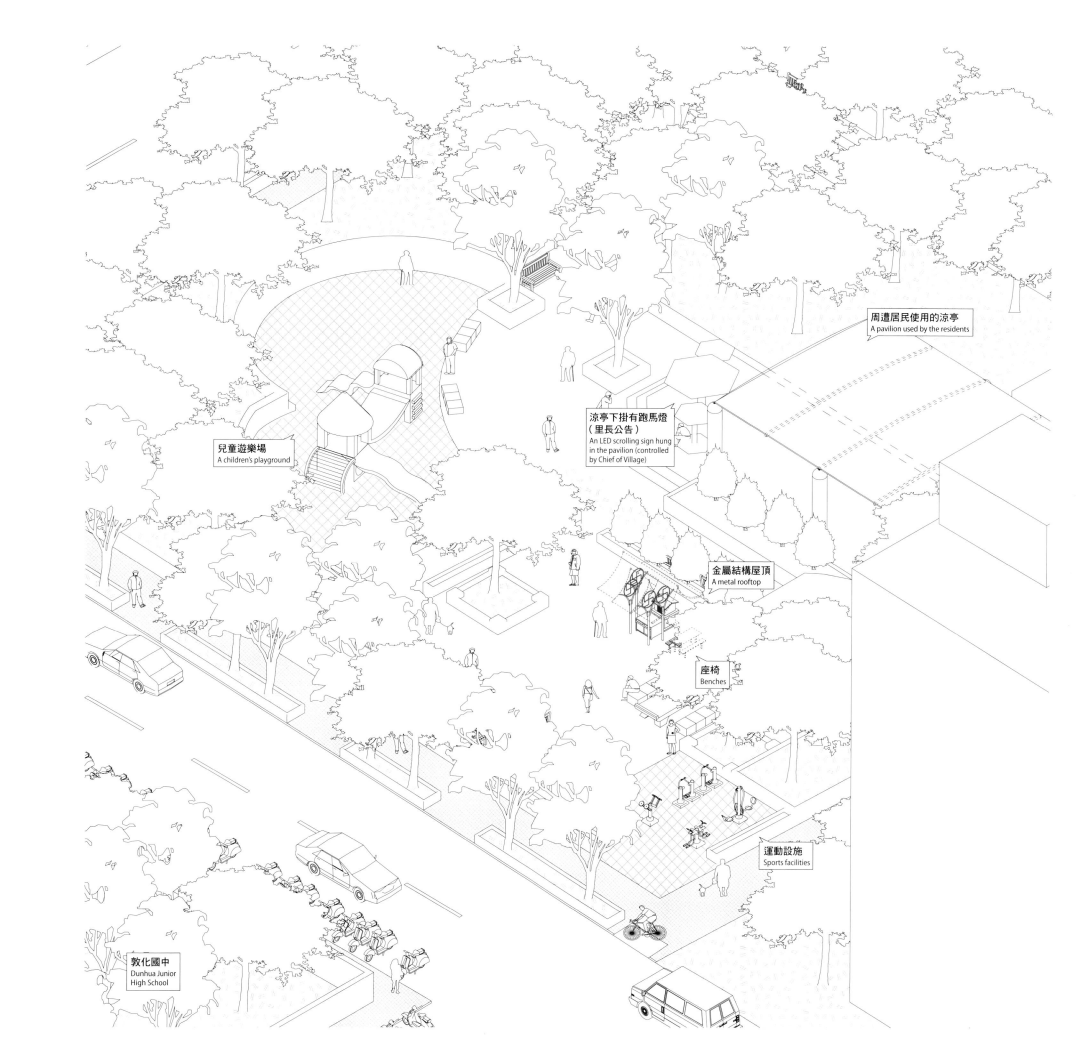

兒童遊樂場
A children's playground

周遭居民使用的涼亭
A pavilion used by the residents

涼亭下掛有跑馬燈
（里長公告）
An LED scrolling sign hung
in the pavilion (controlled
by Chief of Village)

金屬結構屋頂
A metal rooftop

座椅
Benches

運動設施
Sports facilities

敦化國中
Dunhua Junior
High School

35

船廟
Boot Temple

基隆和平島
三府王爺社靈廟

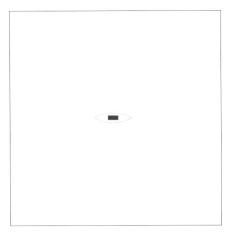

25°09'18.1"N 121°45'54.8"E

XXS

每年農曆的六月十一日，是「社寮島」（和平島舊稱）社靈廟的「遊江河」盛會，不同於其他地區三年一度燒王船以祈求王爺用船將瘟疫載走，三府王爺一年一度巡海遶境，是為了保護漁民海行平安、漁獲大豐收，而王船為王爺的海上坐駕，由漁船拉行出海遊江，遊江後並不燒毀，平日就停放在廟旁供人祭祀。

嚴格來說，船廟大部分時間並非真正寄生於船上，或許不該將其視為寄生之廟。即使有，也只是「游江河」宗教活動與儀式進行時能視為「暫時」寄生於船上。

On the eleventh day of the sixth lunar month every year, a river cruising festival is held in Sheling Temple of Sheliao Island (the old name of Hoping Island). Unlike the tradition practiced in other places where the Wangye boat is burned every three years in the hope of Wangye's shipping the plague away, Sanfu Wangye ("royal lord of three houses") go on a coastal patrol once a year to protect the fishermen at sea and bless them with a good haul.The Wangye boat, Wangye's vehicle on water, is pulled by a fishing boat to cruise around; instead of being burned after the cruise, the boat is placed near the temple for people to worship.

Technically the temple does not really parasitize on the boat most of the time and probably should not be seen as a parasite temple. It can only be temporarily counted as a parasite temple during religious activities and ritual ceremonies like the river cruising festival.

此頁照片均為楊錦煌／攝影

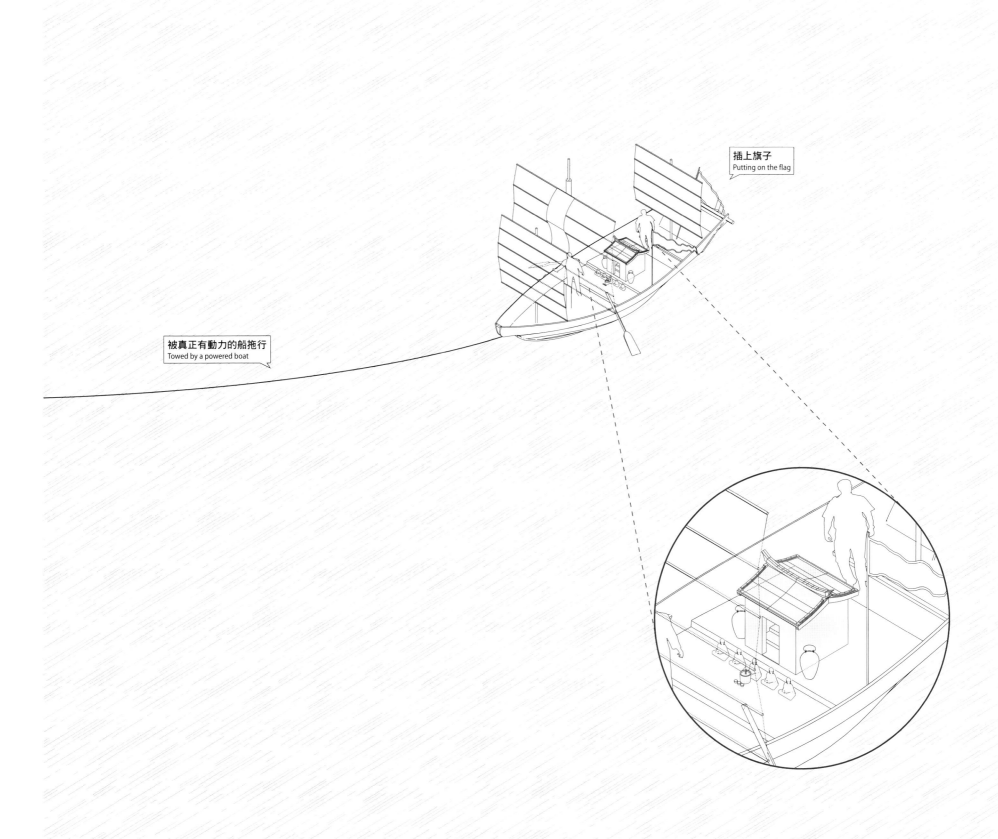

插上旗子
Putting on the flag

被真正有動力的船拖行
Towed by a powered boat

36

打帶跑廟
Run-and-Gun Temple

台北士林百齡寺

25°05'18.3"N 121°30'45.7"E

此廟因不同的落難神祇被居民共同供奉而生。廟體長出四個輪子、像夜市攤販一樣，遇臨檢（特殊狀況）時可隨時推著走。

因為具移動能力，打帶跑廟能以本書中出現過的大部分的宿主為其宿主。在寄生之廟分類學中，可謂「終極」寄生之廟。回應當下這年輕的世代，對廟的信仰需求似乎不再如前一個世代強烈，寄生之廟是否走向式微，也是促使WillipodiA團隊堅持記錄這可能僅見於台灣城市地景遺產的重要原因。

This temple came into existence after several deserted idols were saved and enshrined. Its body grew four wheels like a vending cart in the night market, ready to run when bumping into a police office (or on other special occasions).

Because its mobility, the temple can parasitize upon many of the hosts mentioned in this book. In the taxonomy of parasitic temples, this can be the so-called ultimate. As the devotion to temples is on the decline in younger generations, fear of the fading of the parasitic temples urges WillipodiA to document rare urban landscapes specific to Taiwan.

百齡橋　Bailing Bridge
東西串聯台北市士林區及新北市三重一帶，為社子島重要的對外通道
An important access route connecting Shilin District of Taipei and Sanchong District in New Taipei.

佛具櫃
A ritual item storage cabinet

佛具櫃
A ritual item storage cabinet

唱卡拉OK、下棋的好所在
A good place for karaoke and chess

一對石獅子
A pair of Chinese guardian lions

隱約的參道
An obscure way to the temple

河濱自行車道
The riverside bicycle lane

基隆河
Keelung River

37

一樓七廟
Seven Temples in One Building

台北南機場二期公寓廟群

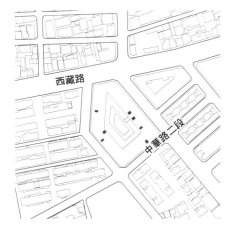

25°01'45.6"N 121°30'14.7"E

南機場二期公寓於1972年完工，為五層樓口字型建築，稱為忠恕社區，為當時公寓住宅的範例。與其說它是個公寓，不如說是個社區，一樓產生許多類型的商業空間：早餐店、理髮店、藥房、柑仔店，甚至是滿足生活所需的福利社。南機場區域為台北市最大的國宅區域，諷刺的是，整建目的是為了安置當時的違建戶，但現今卻成為最大的違章建築區。

當初的整建政策以滿足「量」的需求為主，住戶單元空間相當狹小，其中被夾在住宅單元間的環形長廊，是整個公寓最沒有公共價值的空間，也因此居民開始占用公共空間放洗衣機、冰箱、曬衣服，或往上、往外搭建違建以爭取原本就缺少的生活空間，造就出南機場二期公寓現有的特色，彷彿是環形鳥籠。

多類型的寄生廟隱藏在這口字型建築中，包含三個一樓改造廟、兩個樓中廟及市場廟、屋頂廟各一座。其中最活絡的是中庭對角兩廟，廟埕空間悄悄延伸到環形走廊上，成為居民閒話家常的空間，金爐也因此移至下挖的中庭，它們所屬的廟公不同，但沒有因此產生派系，為常民無神不拜的最佳體現。地下室的果菜市場廟，為當時果菜批發商寄託所留下。此外，隱藏在住宅單元中，並以住宅為單元的廟、佛堂分布在各樓層，平常沒有點燈，大門常關，香爐也從簡擺放在神桌上。一樓七廟的存在，讓居民出入多一份安定感，更是他們生活寄託的空間。

The Second Apartment Building of Nanjichang, aka Zhongxu Community, was completed in 1972. As a five-story building with a courtyard, it was the model of its kind at that time. Rather than an apartment building, it is more like a community. There is a variety of commercial space on the ground floor, including breakfast shops, barbershops, pharmacies and grocery stores to meet the residents' everyday needs. The Nanjichang neighborhood has the largest public housing complex, which was built to accommodate residents of illegal buildings; however, there is now, ironically, the biggest complex of illegal add-ons.

To serve the purpose of relocating in large quantity, maximized number of units make each living quarter cramped, forcing the residents to occupy the public circular corridor to place their washing machines, refrigerators, clothes horses, etc., and to build add-ons upwards or outwards to vie for more space. Those illegally installed window railings and extra floor on the roof have become a notorious signature of the apartment building, making it look like a giant birdcage.

Various parasitic temples hide in the apartment building, including three first-floor-modified temples, two in-between temples, one market temple and one rooftop temple. Two of them facing each other diagonally through the courtyard are the most popular, which extend their squares to the public corridor, where residents gather to chat and gossip; hence the joss paper burners are moved to the courtyard. The market temple in the basement was left by the vendors of the obsolete market. These seven different temples reside in the building, but there are no factions, which is the very embodiment of inclusiveness of folk belief in Taiwan. They hide in units on different floors with lights off and doors closed on normal days and censors simply put on altars. The existence of the seven-in-one temples brings the residents a sense of security.

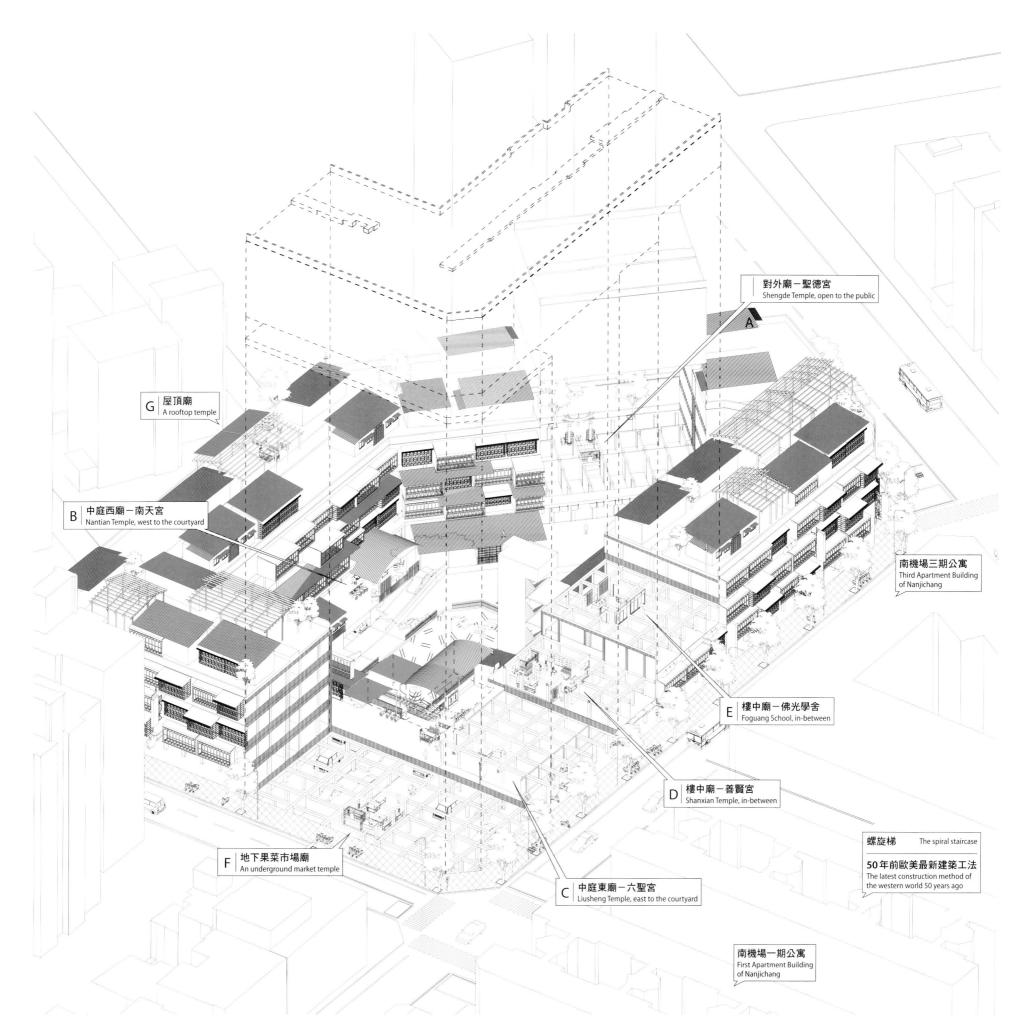

對外廟－聖德宮
Shengde Temple, open to the public

A

G 屋頂廟
A rooftop temple

B 中庭西廟－南天宮
Nantian Temple, west to the courtyard

南機場三期公寓
Third Apartment Building
of Nanjichang

E 樓中廟－佛光學舍
Foguang School, in-between

D 樓中廟－善賢宮
Shanxian Temple, in-between

螺旋梯　The spiral staircase

50年前歐美最新建築工法
The latest construction method of
the western world 50 years ago

F 地下果菜市場廟
An underground market temple

C 中庭東廟－六聖宮
Liusheng Temple, east to the courtyard

南機場一期公寓
First Apartment Building
of Nanjichang

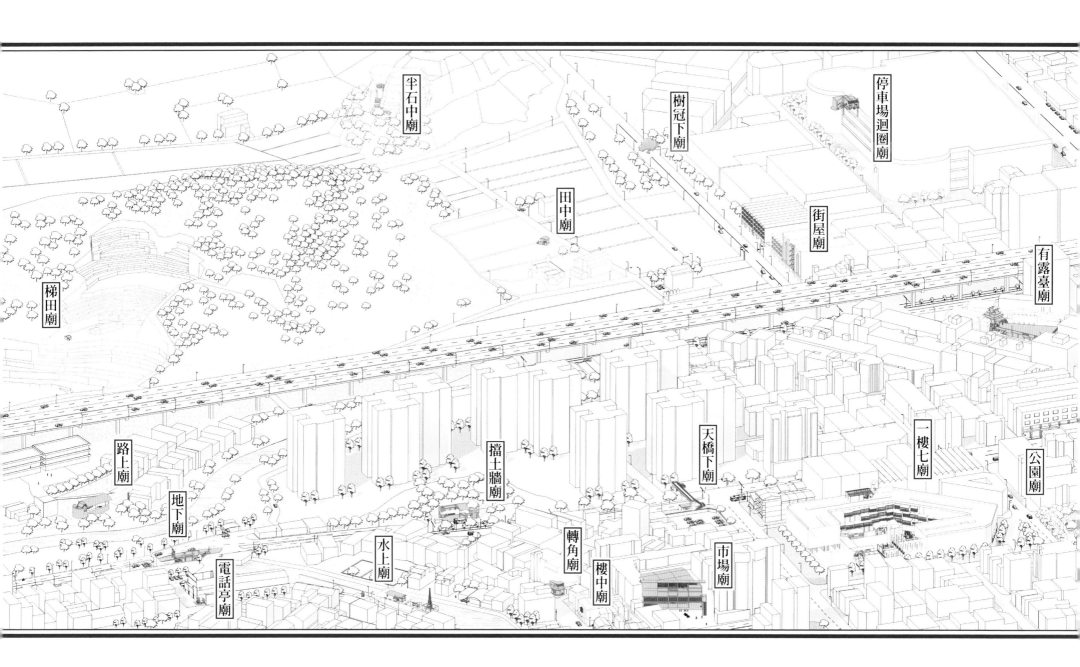

半石中廟
樹冠下廟
停車場迴圈廟
田中廟
街屋廟
有露臺廟
梯田廟
路上廟
擋土牆廟
天橋下廟
一樓七廟
公園廟
地下廟
水上廟
轉角廟
市場廟
電話亭廟
樓中廟

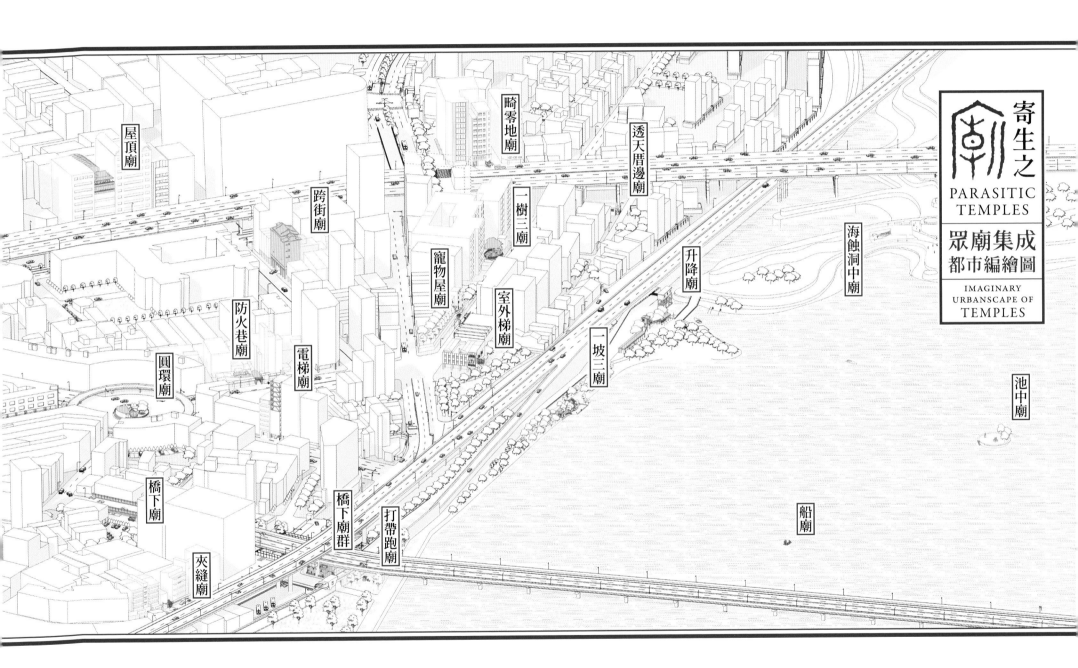

屋頂廟

跨街廟

畸零地廟

透天厝邊廟

一樹三廟

海蝕洞中廟

寵物屋廟

升降廟

防火巷廟

室外梯廟

池中廟

電梯廟

一坡三廟

圓環廟

船廟

橋下廟

橋下廟群

打帶跑廟

夾縫廟

寄生之

廟

PARASITIC
TEMPLES

眾廟集成
都市編繪圖

IMAGINARY
URBANSCAPE OF
TEMPLES

人从众氽

在台灣，無論是小與小、少與少、大與大、多與多的會面場景，皆能連結到一個物件，即是台灣隨處可見的紅色塑膠椅。這物件在這塊土地上不斷出現於廟口、辦桌、小吃攤、嫁娶喜慶、政黨造勢等各類活動。

我們以一種最簡單、最直接、最赤裸，且集體占據空間的形式，讓物件自身建構一個「當我們同在一起」的會面場所。《人从众氽》不是暗示，而是透過「紅椅子」明示了台灣常民文化投射出的認同感與必然性。

團隊成員：
賴伯威、鄧兆旻、何相儀、李佳樺、李齊、康銘展、張淳榕、富田框俊

持之有故，則言之成理

寄生之廟微縮了城市生活型態與紋理，更是紀錄都會變遷過程的活化石。WillipodiA 以類型學的分析方法，建構了寄生之廟的演化系統；我們認為寄生之道既然有跡可循，理應能夠重現，因此與青嵐遊戲製作工作室合作，嘗試以一個規劃經營的桌上遊戲，還原城市與廟共生發展的軌跡。

寄生之廟的遊戲以系統分類中「18族」型態的廟為對象，玩家們每回合交替「廟的寄生」與「土地升級／建設」的動作，讓城市與廟同步進行成長演化；透過規劃經營的過程，讀者、玩家能夠體會這些寄生之廟如何深植城市一隅的邏輯，並理解本書所要傳達：環境決定「天性」、以及演化形塑「個性」的核心概念。

遊戲是本書理論的一項驗證工具，但也同時是獨立的一套休閒娛樂工具；提供讀者一個不同的視角，來感受這些寄生之廟多樣而豐富的魅力。

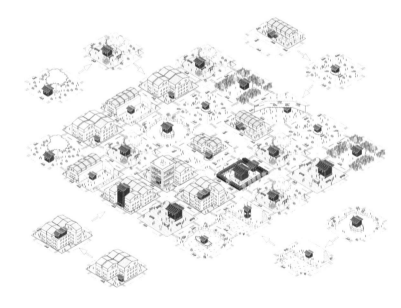

遊戲預計 2018 年春天推出，更多詳情請參考 FB 粉絲專頁

 青嵐遊戲
製作工作室
www.facebook.com/
AoArashiStudio

 WillipodiA
都市研究團隊
www.facebook.com/
willipodia

感謝參與獵廟建模整圖的夥伴們 ─────────────

Honorine Van Den Broek・王鐙德・史可蘋・何相儀・何涵晞・吳宜倫・李佳樺・
李勁蓉・李政嘉・李政儒・李婷珊・林沛錦・林怡邵・林欣慧・林秉翰・林雨湘・
林朗達・邱意婷・高亮慈・張佩珊・曹詠晴・陳乙嬋・陳怡萍・陳弈傑・陳婉宇・
陳詠暄・陳義明・曾睿宏・游宏濤・黃柏硯・黃郁涵・黃皓箴・葉仲之・葉俐琪・
蔡承宇・蔡雅君・蔡聖良・鄭凱蔚・鄭詠倫・賴家豪・戴淯新・薛尹端・謝宜玲（按姓氏筆畫排列）

作　　　者　賴伯威
專案工作團隊　WillipodiA 都市研究團隊
專案執行　Honorine Van Den Broek、何相儀、張佩珊、陳怡萍、陳詠暄、薛尹端
中翻英譯者　林晏生

野人文化股份有限公司
社　　　長　張瑩瑩
總 編 輯　蔡麗真
責任編輯　蔡麗真
行銷企畫　林麗紅
美術設計　黃暐鵬

taste 11 ─────────

寄生之廟
PARASITIC TEMPLES
台灣都市夾縫中的街廟觀察，
適應社會變遷的常民空間圖鑑
（中英對照｜平裝）

出　　　版　野人文化股份有限公司
發　　　行　遠足文化事業股份有限公司（讀書共和國出版集團）
　　　　　　地址：231 新北市新店區民權路 108-2 號 9 樓
　　　　　　電話：(02)2218-1417　傳真：(02)8667-1065
　　　　　　電子信箱：service@bookrep.com.tw
　　　　　　網址：www.bookrep.com.tw
　　　　　　郵撥帳號：19504465 遠足文化事業股份有限公司
　　　　　　客服專線：0800-221-029
法律顧問　華洋法律事務所　蘇文生律師
印　　　製　呈靖彩藝有限公司
初　　　版　2017 年 10 月
二　　　版　2024 年 07 月
定　　　價　800 元
Ｉ Ｓ Ｂ Ｎ　9789863849698（紙本書）
　　　　　　9789863849681（EPUB）
　　　　　　9789863849674（PDF）

國家圖書館出版品預行編目（CIP）資料

寄生之廟：台灣都市夾縫中的街廟觀察，
適應社會變遷的常民空間圖鑑／
賴伯威，WillipodiA 都市研究團隊著.
－初版.－新北市：野人文化出版：
遠足文化發行，2024.07
　　面；　公分.－（Taste；11）；中英對照
ISBN　978-986-384-969-8（平裝）
1.CST: 都市社會學　2.CST: 都市建築
3.CST: 廟宇建築
545.1015　　　　　　　　　112018051

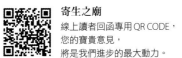

寄生之廟
線上讀者回函專用 QR CODE，
您的寶貴意見，
將是我們進步的最大動力。

諸君所見，非名勝古蹟。
WHAT YOU SEE ARE NOT
HISTORIC MONUMENTS.

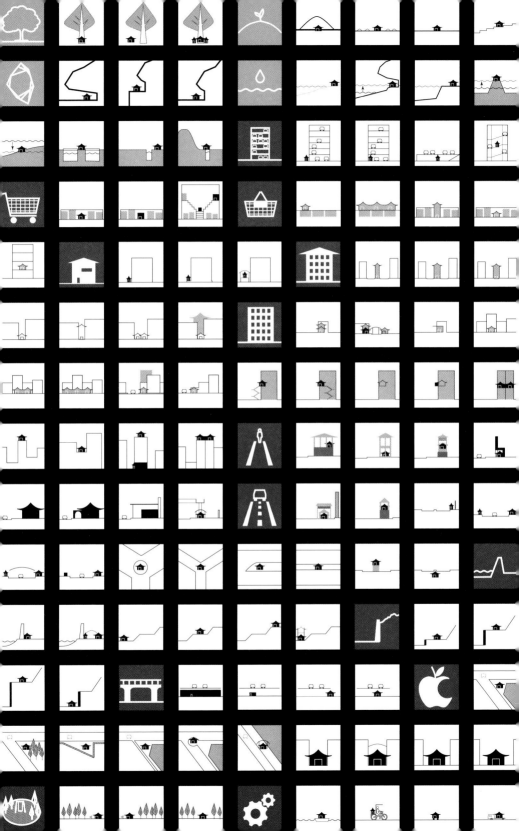